MAID IN SINGAPORE

Maid in Singapore

The serious, quirky and sometimes absurd life of a domestic worker

CRISANTA SAMPANG

Times Editions
Marshall Cavendish

© 2005 Marshall Cavendish International (Asia) Private Limited

Published by Times Editions – Marshall Cavendish
An imprint of Marshall Cavendish International (Asia) Private Limited
A member of Times Publishing Limited
Times Centre, 1 New Industrial Road, Singapore 536196
Tel: (65) 6213 9300   Fax: (65) 6285 4871
E-mail: te@sg.marshallcavendish.com
Online Bookstore: www.marshallcavendish.com/genref

Malaysian Office:
Marshall Cavendish (Malaysia) Sdn Berhad (3024-D)
(General & Reference Publishing)
(Formerly known as Federal Publications Sdn Berhad)
Times Subang
Lot 46, Persiaran Teknologi Subang
Subang Hi-Tech Industrial Park
Batu Tiga, 40000 Shah Alam
Selangor Darul Ehsan, Malaysia
Tel: (603) 5635 2191   Fax: (603) 5635 2706
E-mail: cchong@tpg.com.my

National Library Board (Singapore) Cataloguing in Publication Data

Sampang, Crisanta.
    Maid in Singapore : the serious, quirky and sometimes absurd life of a domestic worker /
Crisanta Sampang. – Singapore : Times Editions-Marshall Cavendish, 2005.

    p. cm.
    ISBN : 981-261-170-3

1. Sampang, Crisanta. 2. Women domestics – Singapore – Biography. 3. Alien labor – Singapore
– Biography. I. Title.

    TX334.1
    640.46092 -- dc21 SLS2005036565

Printed in Singapore

To Maricel, Maricar and Catherine,
my three guardian angels

Contents

Acknowledgements

My sincerest gratitude to my whole extended Singapore family:

To the Aws — Bossy (deceased), Mumsy, Marc and Kenny for welcoming me into the family and for allowing me to share with readers the experiences and adventures I had with them;

To the Hans — Grandpa, Grandma (deceased), Twee Leng, Twee Heng and Loke Kwang. My life has been blessed for having known them;

To Han Fook Kwang and his wife Bee Leng, for all their support and encouragement the whole time I was working on this book, and for their hospitality whenever I stayed in their wonderful home, to their children Ming Chou, Yu Shan and Yu Shi; to their maid Riza.

Special thanks to *The Straits Times* for giving me permission to mine the various articles I have written for the paper during my time in Singapore, for information I used in this book

To the Straits Times' head librarian, Idris Rashid Khan Surattee and his staff, a very helpful bunch of people who assisted me while doing research in the Straits Times Library.

To Wei Fong, Kwang's secretary who guided me around the Strait Times Building while I was researching.

To my children, Maricel, Maricar and Catherine, for reading my drafts, giving their comments and filling out lapses in my memory.

To the women who shared their stories with me and with the readers of this book: Janet Munoz, Rosario Malabanan, and my other friends whom I hope will someday read this book and get in touch again...

To Mrs Merriam Cuasay, who contributed her knowledge and own experiences with Filipino maids, validating my observations.

To my Canadian friends, who, in one way or another, encourage me with kind words and emotional support: Daniel Wood, Steve Knopp, Cynthia Javier, Kerry Banks, April Saunders and Jess Hennan.

To my employers, Hugh and Donna Tangye, for their understanding and flexibility in allowing me to take time off whenever necessary to complete this project.

And finally, to my editor, Melissa Heng, who showed patience and understanding that would rival that of Job, and who allowed my voice to come clearly through the pages of this book.

1987.
REMEMBERING IMELDA.

I can't even recall her name. I call her Imelda now. She told me she couldn't bear the thought of going back to her hometown of Santa Clara, in Batangas, Philippines, a failure. Her parents depended on her for their livelihood. They had sold the carabao they used to till the farm and her father had borrowed money from the bank using the farm as collateral — all this just so that they could pay the agency that brought her to Singapore. She needed to find another employer right away. If she didn't, her parents could lose the farm.

I promised Imelda that I would help her find a new job, but for now, she needed some rest. I assured her there were a lot of employers out there who would be only too happy to hire a nanny without having to pay an agency fee. Before I left her that night, I told Mr Fred Rosario, the Philippines' Labour Attaché to Singapore, that I thought Imelda needed to see a doctor. She did not look well and would need some medication to calm her down. Mr Rosario agreed with my observation. He took her to the hospital himself the next day.

Nine years — and two deaths later — I was forced to think about Imelda again, and to recall the desperate loneliness that Filipino women face when leaving family and home to work in a different country. For each of us, isolation and the lack of emotional support are the most common problems. In a foreign place, it's not easy finding someone to talk to. And when one does find a listener, it may already be too late.

I met Imelda, a domestic worker, at the Philippines Community Centre in Singapore. She was 23 years old then, about 4'10" (1.47 m) and looked much younger than her age. Her employer had dropped her off at the Centre because she had apparently been incapable of working. Instead of doing her tasks, Imelda would sit in her room and cry all day. To all appearances, Imelda had a mental breakdown.

The Centre where Imelda stayed was built in 1987 by then president, Cory Aquino, in response to requests by Filipino workers in Singapore for a place of recreation. It was meant to be a place where maids could hang out on weekends. It was also meant to serve as a shelter for those who were in-between jobs. Mr Fred Rosario was the person-in-charge of the Centre.

I remember visiting the Centre quite often. Talking to other Filipinos had helped ease my own homesickness.

It was on a Sunday evening that Mr Rosario asked me if I could talk to Imelda. Imelda and I came from the same province and he thought I might be able to give her some comfort. She had just arrived at the Centre and had looked terribly upset. Imelda was sitting by herself in one corner, endlessly wringing a handkerchief in her hands. Her puffy eyes told me she had been crying for some time.

The girl was very scared. She was worried that she wouldn't find another job.

"Please, please, can you help me? I don't know what to do anymore," she had pleaded with me. Imelda told me how frightened she was of her employer's brother. Each time the brother got drunk, he would threaten her with a knife, saying, "You are nothing. If I kill you right now, no one would care."

Imelda believed him.

Mr Rosario called me the next morning informing me that he had taken Imelda to the hospital for a check up. The doctor had requested that she stay overnight for observation. Having assisted in the paperwork required for admission, Mr Rosario left the hospital. Out in the parking lot, while walking to his car, he heard a loud thud. He turned, and saw Imelda on the ground. She had jumped from the fourth floor window of the hospital.

I did not see Imelda the day she died. It was a bright, sunny morning when Mr Rosario called to tell me about her death. I was getting my family's lunch ready, happily humming a tune while picking roots off some bean sprouts. I was cooking Hokkien Mee that day. All I recalled was me saying "Oh" in response. The Embassy would send her body home.

Looking back now, I realised how little I knew about Imelda. Which hospital she went to; when her remains were sent home, who her parents were, etc. I never found out how Mr Rosario felt, seeing Imelda dead on the ground. I did not really know what to say. As he was telling me what happened, I was thinking about the parents who had pinned so much hope and expectations upon the dead woman. What a sad homecoming it was going to be. She had told me that she was their sole ticket out of poverty. That was a big responsibility. I prayed that her parents who had lost a daughter would not lose their livelihood as well. And I prayed even harder that I would forget the whole incident, because I had lost the chance to help, and I did not have the heart to dwell upon it any further.

Like other bad memories, I swept Imelda under the carpet. I was happy to go back to picking roots off my bean sprouts. I forgot about Imelda.

Not long after, Mr Rosario asked for — and was granted — a transfer to another country. We staged a big farewell party for him. It didn't occur to me then that witnessing Imelda's suicide could have so traumatised the man that he wanted to leave. After all, Singapore wasn't a bad place to live and work in.

Years passed. I moved to Vancouver in Canada, where I worked first as a volunteer, then as a paid staff, in a non-profit organisation that helped foreign domestic workers resolve their immigration or employment problems. In the course of my job, I came across two more suicides. One of them was a close friend. The year was 1995.

My friend Gloria was a volunteer at the organisation. She was a kind and cheerful woman — always smiling, always ready to help out during special functions. Like Imelda, Gloria was carrying an emotional load too heavy for her to bear, but she never talked about it. Gloria had been working in Vancouver as a nanny for four years. Throughout that time, she worked very hard, sending most of her money home and saving up the rest. She had spent all her savings and borrowed a bit more to bring her husband, Ramon, and their teenaged daughter, Daisy, to Vancouver. The sponsorship fees and airfares had cost her CAD$4,000. This was no mean sum for a nanny, whose monthly salary averaged CAD$1,000. Gloria was going broke because of all the bills she had to pay on a nanny's wage.

One Tuesday morning, Gloria called to ask me for help in finding her husband a job. Ramon was 47. He had been in Vancouver for six months and was still unemployed. He had been looking for work — any kind of work — but wasn't able to find any. According to Gloria, Ramon was feeling increasingly frustrated and depressed. The weather didn't help. It was autumn in Vancouver, cold and rainy. When it wasn't raining, the sky was overcast. They were living in a small, one-bedroom basement suite with their daughter. Again, I promised to do everything I could to help. I told her I would have job leads for her by Saturday.

Two days later, on Thursday, the phone rang. It was Ramon. He said, "Gloria is dead. She had told me before that if I ever needed help, I should call you."

Once again, I did not know how to respond. I only managed to ask him for their address. I closed the office, got into my car and drove around the city aimlessly for hours, trying to muster some courage before facing Ramon. I felt hurt, angry, but most of all, guilty. Recollections of Imelda started coming back to me.

Imelda had also asked me for help. I had promised to help her, but she couldn't wait. I didn't know if she even believed me. But Gloria was different. She was my friend. We had worked together side by side at many fundraising events. She had always given me a hug whenever we met. She was one of my favourite volunteers. But before that phone call on Tuesday, I had known nothing about her personal problems. Gloria could have at least given me a chance to help her.

Not too long after Gloria died, I left my job, or lost it — I didn't care which. I had lost my passion for the work. I had lost my self-confidence. I made mistakes. Before all the suicides, I had felt young. I was full of hope, and I had high ideals. I believed I could change lives. Like Hercules, I thought I had enough strength to carry the world on my shoulders.

I was wrong.

People died on my watch, and I had no clue it was going to happen. I felt old, useless, guilty, and definitely in the wrong profession. Was there anything I could have done to prevent Imelda's and Gloria's suicides? Had I listened longer, asked more questions, could the fates of these two people have played out differently? If I hadn't repressed the memory of Imelda's death, could I have better understood Gloria's situation and offered positive help before it was too late?

Since then, I've thought a lot about the subject of suicide. I've researched it. I've downloaded information about it from the Internet. Yet, it had taken me years to write these thoughts down. It's a purging, if you will, of the darkness that lurked in my psyche. A vacuuming of bad memories I've accumulated under the carpet.

Why did I run away from these painful recollections? It's hard to explain. Those women's deaths were born of pain, and I wasn't able to make a difference. That knowledge was hurting. I've always felt like a sponge in the presence of suffering, absorbing other people's anger or frustrations, making their problems my own. And I suffer because of it. I can't even watch a documentary on starving children because it gives me nightmares. I only watch movies with happy endings. I look away when a homeless person digs something out of a dumpster and starts eating it. I couldn't bring myself to look misery in the eye — because I knew all too well what misery means.

I still try to imagine, every now and then, what Imelda had been thinking in the final seconds of her life, before she jumped. What could have gone on in her mind that so frightened her that made her choose death over hope?

I need to lay Imelda's ghost to rest. I need to return to Singapore.

This is my story — a story not of one person, but of countless others like me, who had left both hearth and home in the hope of finding a better life abroad. Some of us luckier ones found it, eventually.

Many others did not.

Let me walk you down this winding road, so that you, too, may begin to understand some of the joys and pains of working as a domestic in a foreign land.

THE WAY THINGS WERE

My aunt took the wet cleaning cloth from me, wrapped a corner of it around her index finger, and began attacking the dust all along the edge of a wooden staircase. She rubbed it carefully until all the dirt disappeared.

"There," she said. "That's how you clean a house. Look for dirt in every corner, and go after it, like so!"

It was the 1960s. I was nine years old. I have never seen or heard of a vacuum cleaner. Wanting to please, I listened closely to my aunt and applied her instructions conscientiously. I didn't know it then, but her housekeeping tips were to play a very important part in my life as a domestic worker.

I was born in Lipa, a farming town in the province of Batangas, about 100 kilometres south of Manila. My father was a rice farmer, and we owned a track of land that he tilled and planted with different crops all year round. We had a variety of fruit trees and bamboo in our orchards. At any one time, we had two or three cows, several pigs, goats and chickens roaming around our yard. We also had two dogs and at least seven cats. There was a creek running at the edge of the farm where Mother washed our clothes and my brothers took the cows to drink. I learned to swim in the deeper sections of this creek— the same places where Father and I went to set his crab and shrimp traps in the evenings.

I loved that little creek.

When my family first moved to the farm (before I was born), Father had dug a spring well in its western bank, protected by overhanging trees. We would get our drinking water from this tiny spring. It was a time before sugar cane farmers took over and clogged up the waterways with their sugar cane cuttings; before discarded plastic bags became a permanent eyesore littering the area. We did not have electricity, irrigation or sewage systems. We had an outhouse, but if the need arose when you were away from home, you went into the bush.

I remembered having a relatively happy childhood. I had everything I ever wanted. My mind then was unpolluted by television. Money was an unknown quantity. I had books and I had pets. My imagination provided whatever else was lacking and it helped me create my own perfect world. It was a magical time that lasted all of nine years. When I turned nine, my childhood ended.

Where I grew up, school only went up to the fourth grade. We had two school rooms in an old building, where Grades One & Two were combined in one and Grades Three & Four were held in the other. After Grade Four, girls stayed home to help their mothers with housework, while boys worked with their fathers on the farms, or hang out with their friends when farming season was over. My parents didn't have much money, but we had enough food to go around. We had a close network of friends and relatives. When money was needed, Father would sell a portion of the harvest or livestock.

Houses were built and fields were weeded, harvested and prepared for the next planting season with the help of the whole community. Every farmer scheduled his farm work in consultation with the others, so that everyone would get the help they needed during the course of the season.

Those were carefree years. Young people had plenty of time for group activities, like celebrating a patron saint's feast day and all other public holidays. I used to tag behind my big sister, my big brothers and all their friends, especially during the month of May. We would collect wild flowers around the farm and use these to ˙ ~orate the village chapel for the month-long nightly offering of sor to the Virgin Mary. Or we would be out caroling durin fundraising on All Soul's Day.

Being out of school, many young people ma marriageable age ranged from 13 to 19 years, an reached the age of 25 without being married, she would be considered an old maid.

In those days, nobody from my village ever went away to another city to work or study. Farmers would go as far as Manila to sell their fruit and vegetables but would come back after three days. No one worked as a domestic, or *katulong*, as they called these household helpers.

We lived in Luzon, the largest of the Philippines' 7,100 islands. Manila and Quezon City, the country's business centres, are located in Luzon. People from other islands and remote provinces were drawn to our cities, particularly to Manila. Most of these migrant workers were from the Visayan Islands or the Ilocos region. They were all adventurous, hardworking people who were not afraid to leave their comfort zones to build a better future for themselves. Every domestic or houseboy we knew was from the Visayas, so much so that the name *bisaya* became synonymous with hired help. It wasn't derogatory; it just seemed to us farm folks that while the Ilocanos become farm workers or small businessmen, the Visayans tend to work inside the homes.

Back then, the Philippines was an agricultural country rich in natural resources. Timber, minerals, and rich farmlands helped provide for every need. As I grew older, however, things started to change. Ferdinand Marcos had been president of the Philippines for as far as I could remember, and everyone said the country was getting poorer the longer he stayed in office. In 1972, he declared martial law and things got worse. He appointed his friends to key positions in the government, and the national debt grew exponentially. The value of the peso went downhill, from two pesos to one US dollar, to twenty five to one by the time I was old enough to work. Jobs became scarce, and there was a glut of university graduates who couldn't find employment.

After the dust cleared, the masses settled back into their poverty — a situation that encouraged everyone to look for a livelihood outside of the country. Doctors, nurses, engineers, and other professionals powered the first wave of the Filipino brain-drain. These poured into hospitals, oil fields and construction sites in foreign lands. Domestic workers followed the same path to Hong Kong, Singapore, Italy and the Middle East. Where there was a need for international workers, there were Filipinos hoping to fill them. By 1985, there were over four million Filipinos working abroad, providing services in exchange for dollars to support the families they left behind.

When my turn to leave the country came, I was ready. If others could do it, so could I. Besides, it couldn't possibly be much worse than being sent off to the city to live when I was but a tiny kid, who had previously been a princess in my own realm, peopled with a dozen pets and a host of imaginary friends. Before all these, I hardly ever lifted a finger to help with chores. My daily activities outside of school consisted of reading, napping, climbing trees and playing with family pets. Then suddenly, I was living with other people, most of whom I've never met before. My status took a plunge. There was no one I could relate to, except the female *bisaya* in the house who happened to be really nice to me. If I could survive such a traumatic change at age nine, I believed I could survive anything in my adulthood.

How did all this came about?

My parents sent me to the city to study after I graduated from Grade Four in the village school. My teachers believed I was a very smart child and that with good education, my future would be assured. My father agreed. He had always wanted me to become a schoolteacher. A schoolteacher was highly respected in our village and everyone who hoped to go to college aspired to become one. There were only three teachers there during my childhood and they were all held in the highest regard. People address them as Mr Lirag, Mrs Laylo, or Miss Atienza. Nobody called them by their first names, ever. My father hoped I could be just like one of them.

So off I went to the city. I boarded with my father's relatives. In the city, I soon learned to clean the house, cook, wash my own clothes;

learned to accept that I was now one of the lesser individuals in a new environment. My young brain couldn't comprehend why I had to live with these people. I condemned my parents for sending me away. For the next 18 years, until my arrival in Singapore, I considered myself an orphan, visiting my parents only on holidays. I was convinced that I had raised myself. I drifted through my teenage years without purpose, and whatever intelligence my parents believed I possessed was all wasted. I dropped out of college in my third year, and got married the year after.

By early 1984, I was restless. My husband and I were living in another town then. We had three young daughters. My husband was a thriving businessman with a fondness for imported whisky. He would spend many nights drinking with his friends. But he was hard working. To all appearances, we were a happy young family. We were popular, we loved each other, and we were reasonably well off.

Nobody knew the unhappiness that simmered beneath my seemingly contented life. I felt useless, trapped, with no place to go. Praying was not even an option. I had dropped that habit when, as a child, I felt that God was not listening to me. I was not unlike one of Hemingway's characters from the story, *A Clean Well-lighted Place*, chanting a meaningless mantra to a non-existent self: "Our nada, who art in nada, hallowed be thy nada..."

Even as I sat there on the front steps of my house, chatting with other young wives, comparing notes about our children and the price of groceries, I would silently wonder why I was so unhappy, why being married and jobless, waiting daily for my husband to come home from work, or from his nights out with the boys, did not seem like the happily-ever-after story that I had envisioned married life to be. There was something else out there for me, but I did not know what it was. I felt myself drowning, weighted down by daily routine, and all I could do was try to surface as often as I could to fill my lungs with air. My only joy seemed to come from watching my little girls grow up.

The drowning feeling continued, aggravated by my husband's growing addiction to alcohol. There were days when he would start chugging beer early in the morning, a session that would go on until the next day. Sometimes, the drinking threatened to turn rowdy. Nobody thought it bad or unusual, because in Batangas, sharing an alcoholic beverage was a normal social activity for macho men, especially if you could afford it. I, on the other hand, raged silently against such drinking parties. If there was something in life I loathed more than anything else, it was watching a member of my family succumb to alcohol, then make a fool of himself — scenarios I had repeatedly observed growing up. My brothers drank. My father would think he was superman after a few shots of gin, and despite the great affection we shared for each other, I often felt that I didn't really know him each time he was drunk.

I was slowly growing apart from my husband. If he noticed, he didn't acknowledge it. Everything came to a head one day, after he went over to his brother's place and failed to come home that night. It was New Year's Eve, and we had a table loaded with *media noche* fare ("media noche" is what Filipinos call New Year's Eve dinner, and it's eaten at midnight, after the year changes). There was *pancit*, loaves of bread, different types of fruit, marinated pieces of pork and chicken for the barbecue, and imported cheese. We had firecrackers ready to be lighted. The Eve came and went and the food turned cold. The firecrackers remained in their plastic wrappers. My ears were trained all night towards the sound of vehicles stopping near the house, dogs barking, and someone getting off, but he didn't turn up. My mother was visiting us at the time, and I was offended that he showed her such disregard. In my mind, that was an unforgivable act.

I found out later that he actually tried to come home, but was too drunk and passed out on the roadside after getting off the passenger jeepney.

That New Year morning, a neighbour found him fast asleep on a grassy spot by the road, when the man went out early to pasture his goats. The neighbour came to report this to me. My mother was shaken. She asked the neighbour if my husband was still alive. The man wasn't sure. My mother nagged me to go and see him but I refused.

In the end, my mother and a few of our neighbours walked over and woke him up. Life was never the same after that.

Two months later, I decided that I have had enough. We agreed to separate.

I packed my children and my belongings and went home to Mother. I had nothing else except my family, but at that time, they were all I needed.

ONE-WAY TICKET

So this was me in the spring of 1984 — I was 27, without a husband, without a job, and with three small kids to feed. I was too short to work in a factory and too inexperienced to work in an office. I had never worked on a farm. Neither did I know anyone influential enough to help me get a job anywhere else. I wanted to write, but my world was too limited and I had nothing original to say. Somehow, selling my body never occurred to me. So I set my sight further. Driven by necessity and armed with the knowledge that dirt lay in wait on every staircase, I felt confident that all I needed was an accurate index finger wrapped around a wet piece of cleaning cloth. Thus did I embarked on a new adventure — working abroad as a domestic.

I knew that wherever I was going, life would be better than where I was. I only hoped that my daughters would understand why I had to let them grow up without me.

By this time, my family had sold the farm, my father had passed away, and my brother Fernando supported my mother. Now, he also had to look after my children and me. In my village, you don't take a husband to court for child support. If someone had ever done it before, nobody talked about it. An ex-wife should be happy if she received something; anything. I received nothing.

But even though I had nothing to show for it, I had big dreams. I promised myself that my three little girls would never grow up like me, sent away to some city and left in the care of strangers, bereft of family and material things. I would provide for them everything that they needed. Not having a wristwatch or a new toy may seem trivial to a grown-up, but such things are important to a child, especially if she is surrounded by others who have all these things. They were important to me when I was growing up in the city, which was a very materialistic place. Having a huge, colourful wristwatch like those my classmates

23

wore would have made me felt, in today's lingo, *cool*. Being merely smart didn't cut it. It was all about belonging. You needed shiny leather shoes, well-cut school uniforms and a regular allowance so you could go to the canteen with your friends. I had none of those.

I vowed that my children would have these stuff; they would be cool, popular, and surrounded by people who love them.

I promised I would never let them feel what I had felt when I was a kid, clutching at my blankie and crying into my little pillow, in a strange bedroom, with unfamiliar folks. But I needed an income if I were to fulfill my promise.

I looked around for work. I scanned the employment section of the papers everyday, hoping an opportunity would turn up. I've always been an optimist. I believe that life is constantly changing. It always gets better — or worse — depending on what state one is in. In my case, it could only get better. One day, I spotted an advertisement recruiting domestic workers for Singapore. The agency was called MS Catan, based in Malate, MetroManila At that very moment, I saw my ship sail into the horizon. This is it, I thought — the passport to my dreams.

Early the next day, I went off to MS Catan to apply for the job. The place was overflowing with women. I joined the long queue, got myself an application form and filled it out. A question in the form asked for my marital status. If the applicant was married, a written permission from the husband was required. A written permission? No way! Although separated from my husband, I was still considered legally married; but I wasn't about to crawl back to a drunken, bitter ex-husband, nor let him prevent me from pursuing my destiny. So I lied, shoved my guilty feelings way deep where I wouldn't find them again, and presented myself as a single woman. What I did has never stopped bothering me, but at the time, I did not have much choice. I was desperate. So I kept reminding my Machiavellian self that my past deeds would be justified by what I would later achieve.

After the interview, they gave me a list of things I needed to produce

— police and National Bureau of Investigation security clearances, along with dental and medical certifications that I was healthy enough to work abroad. All these things required cash. I went home and sold my TV set, my Omega watch and my jewelry. I was all right for the time being.

You have to understand; going abroad to work is not for the truly poor or the chicken-hearted. To afford the expense, farm folks like me would sell their farm animals; use their farms as collateral to borrow money from the bank, or approach loan sharks for quick loans. Loan sharking is common in the Philippines. It's not an enterprise run by some Filipino Mafia, but by your friendly, neighbourhood, five-six moneylender, someone who comes around every day to collect your installment fees. A five-six debt is like a relentlessly ticking taxi-meter. For every 100 pesos you borrowed, you pay an interest of twenty pesos a month. If you failed to pay regular dues and the unpaid interest reaches a certain amount, it's added to the principal loan and then you start paying interest on that as well.

You don't get your legs broken for missing payments. You just get deeper into debt, and unless you start earning dollars, you'll be paying installments well into your old age.

I was fortunate that my family had nothing to sell or use as collateral, so I avoided incurring a huge debt when I was getting ready to work in a foreign country. I had no prospects. No one, not even my mother nor my cousins, believed that I would ever get off the ground. The local loan shark wouldn't touch me.

I did not hold this against them. During the last 18 years of my life, I hadn't exactly been communicative, or reliable, or anchored in any way. I did whatever I wanted — ran away from my aunt's home at the age of 11; dropped out of college at 18 despite a government scholarship, then got pregnant before getting married, perhaps to spite my parents.

All these things I had done in the past were now coming back to haunt me.

No one in my family knew or understood that becoming a parent had irrevocably altered my perspective. I never talked about it.

There was one other reason why people in my village couldn't believe that applying for work abroad was as easy as I made it out to be — nobody in the village before me had ever gone to Manila to do it on his own. The few who were now in Saudi Arabia or Hong Kong used middlemen and paid thousands of pesos before they were able to leave the country. Many of those who had spent huge amounts of money were still waiting to go, even as everybody else knew that they never would. These were the ones who got "faked" — foreign worker wannabes who had blindly trusted unscrupulous recruiters, who, in turn, took off with the applicants' money and never came back.

It was sad, but the next applicant always believed that his agent would be more dependable. In a few cases, they actually had passports to show for it. My village had a number of such unlucky individuals.

So there I was, running around to get my application package together, when one day, I came home to find my brother Fernando in bed with broken bones. A drunk driver — a cousin from the same place — had rammed his jeepney into my brother the night before. His friends found him in a crumpled heap in a ditch beside the road. In cases like these, nobody went to the police. The village people usually sort these things out by appointing a representative, usually a respected elder known to both parties, or an influential relative to act as a go-between. This was done to avoid worsening the situation, when vendetta could land other members of both families in jail, or worse, in a hospital.

A delegation from the driver's family met with my brother and mother to ask for forgiveness and to offer some financial compensation. They suggested seven thousand pesos, an amount the other party felt would tide my brother over his recuperation period and pay for his hospital bills. This was a gesture of goodwill.

My family accepted the offer and considered the whole thing settled.

I was too angry and too mired in my own problems to get involved in the discussions.

A few weeks later, I completed the requirements and was told by the agency that I now had an employer waiting for me in Singapore. The agency's Singaporean counterpart will pay for the airline ticket and deduct it from my pay once I started working. All I needed to do was pay them one thousand pesos to finalise my application. This was an amount I did not have. I went home and requested my mother to let me sell our last cow, but she refused. She had promised it to my other brother, an electrician who wanted to start a snack shop at his workplace in Manila.

I did not argue, or beg. I walked away quietly, and when I thought I was far enough from my mother, I picked up a broken plastic toy and hurled it against a wooden post. As I watched the pieces fall to the ground, my bedridden brother called me into his room.

It was a scene, a conversation, that would remain clear in my mind for the rest of my life. As I stood there in front of him, he asked me: "How much do you need?"

I told him, "You can't do this. You need your money to get better."

He said, "I have enough for now. And besides, you'll pay me back when you get there, won't you?"

I didn't protest. My heart was breaking as I watched him take his settlement money from under his pillow and counted out two thousand pesos.

"That should help you until you fly out."

I accepted the loan gratefully, with a solemn promise to him and to myself — "I will never let you down, *Kuya*."

I went back to MS Catan and paid my fees. The placement staff told me to go home and wait to be called back. They would send me a telegram when it was my turn to go. I checked in by calling long distance once a week to see if I had a flight schedule. I was disappointed every time. This went on for four weeks. Everyone was whispering that I had been faked behind my back. My *Kuya*, God bless him, said nothing. His trust in me remained unshaken.

Talking to people whose relatives had gone abroad gave me an insight into what I called "employment agency economics". Apparently, agencies here do not buy regular airline tickets. They send their people out as "chance passengers" instead. These chance seats cost half the price of regular ones. The agencies then wait for the airline to call in the number of remaining seats on flights leaving that day, and proceed to contact those who are ready to leave.

MS Catan had a number of workers with their luggage all packed and on stand-by in the office daily. These women were practically camped there and could fly at a moment's notice. This I found out after hanging around the agency one day. With this newly acquired knowledge, I sought out the head dispatcher and introduced myself. I had to make sure she would remember me. So I went home, bought some young coconut pies — a delicacy in my area — and went back to the agency the next day. I distributed my pies and bought the whole office a round of Coca Cola. I re-introduced myself and told them how important it was for me to be able to leave soon. The person-in-charge wrote my name down and told me, "Crisanta, bring your bags tomorrow. You're flying at four o'clock."

One line from a crucial gate-keeper made all the difference. In a matter of seconds, the whole world had opened up to me. I mumbled my thanks, ran out of MS Catan's office, and did a jig on my way to the bus stop.

Back home, I put a few pieces of clothing together, my toothbrush, one pair of shoes, a pair of slippers, my passport, and a US twenty dollar bill that I had been saving as pocket money. I told my brother and my mother that I would be going the next morning. I was in a state of shock the whole night — neither sad nor excited, just numb. I cuddled my daughters and looked at them one by one — Maricel was almost seven and had started going to school; Maricar was five; and Catherine was two. I want to remember how they looked like when I leave them. I would not see my girls for two years. I knew my mother would care for them, but I also knew I would greatly regret not being around while they were growing up.

Early the next morning, I put my things in a plastic shopping bag. I woke up the girls and kissed each of them goodbye.

The poor children had no idea what was happening. My mother slung Catherine around her waist and followed me out. Maricel and Maricar walked alongside her. I walked ahead towards the jeepney with my plastic bag. I left early because I was stopping by in the next town, where I would borrow a small luggage from my cousin, Norma.

As I settled into my seat in the jeepney, I waved to my mother and the girls. Mother said, "Take care, little girl. May God go with you." The neighbours stood around my mother and asked where I was going. Mother said, "She's leaving for Singapore today."

"All by herself?" I saw everybody's jaw drop when my mother nodded. Ordinarily, going overseas was a festive occasion. The family would spread the word around, a big goodbye party would be held, and then a fleet of jeepneys loaded with relatives would send the worker off at the Manila International Airport. But this morning wasn't anywhere near festive. I was going by myself to the airport.

The jeepney revved up, and I watched my family and the neighbours slowly disappear behind a cloud of dust.

SINGAPORE AHOY!

I left the Philippines for the first time in my life in July, 1984. I flew with six other women who had all been placed by MS Catan, in partnership with Humana Pte Ltd in Singapore. The two other married women in my group cried throughout the flight, sniffling softly into their hankies.

Like both of them, it was my first time leaving my children without really knowing when I would be back. I wasn't sure what kind of life lay before me in Singapore. I had no idea how my daughters would react to my long absence. I probably felt just as homesick as any one of these women, but somehow, shedding tears didn't come easy for me. I guess my tear ducts dried up when I was a kid, having cried my eyes out back then. Right now, sadness just felt like a load of rocks sitting on my chest, preventing me from breathing, and leaving me incapable of making small talk. But apart from the pain of separation, I felt no regret. And not much fear either. I was determined to make this trip work.

Before leaving the Philippines, I had signed a two-year contract that, among other things, provided for a monthly salary of S$300, with free board and lodging.That was worth about 2,400 pesos, at the exchange rate of eight pesos to the Singapore dollar. That, of course, was before the inflation of the peso. I would not be receiving any salary, however, until the full price of my air ticket had been paid. In addition to this, a further S$450 dollars would be deducted from my pay to cover any emergencies, such as a return flight ticket if my assignment in Singapore didn't work out, or if I had to leave before my contract was up. Should I successfully complete my contract term, my employers would pay for my air ticket home. I thought that was a fair arrangement.

I also signed a statute of undertaking once I arrived in Singapore, promising that I would not get pregnant, cohabit with, or marry, a Singaporean; or get involved in any illegal activities. I would also not work for any other employer except the one named in my work permit. All these besides, I was to undergo a pregnancy test every six months. I signed everything. It had seemed fair to me — I was going to another country to work. I had no intention of getting pregnant. It was a privilege to be here, and I was not about to question how other people run their country.

My bosses, Mr and Mrs Aw Kum Jin, had their share of obligations in the agreement. They posted a bond of S$5,000 as a guarantee that I, the maid, would honour everything that I have signed, and to make sure that I stayed out of trouble while in Singapore. They were also required to pay a monthly levy of S$120 for the right to employ a domestic.

On the way in, my group and I stopped over for a night in Hong Kong, before continuing on to Singapore. It was a Friday when we arrived. As the plane descended towards Changi International Airport, I looked down and saw a land with reddish soil, streets lined with trees, and numerous clusters of tall buildings grouped around what looked like little green parks. I mentally noted all these observations. It was important to me to remember every detail of my arrival.

A representative of Humana met us at the airport and loaded us into two taxis. I looked out the window as soon as I settled into my seat. The sight did not disappoint. Whole lines of tall, green trees flanked the roads on both sides, their overhanging branches providing shade and creating an illusion of restfulness despite the busy traffic. Where there were no trees, flowering shrubs and grassy patches took over. I was amazed at the city's cleanliness and orderliness. There was not a scrap of dirty paper, no rusty cans, nor used plastic bags littering the sidewalks. Someone, I thought, had taken pains to look after this place.

We went directly to Humana's apartment in the Katong area, where we spent the weekend. A man, whose name I have forgotten, was put in-charge of the apartment and all incoming maids. His job was to welcome and orientate us. That night, we slept on plastic mats on the living room floor. The ceiling lights made it hard for me to fall asleep, so I covered my eyes with my hand towel. The man in-charge, who had come to check on us, noticed my appearance and said to me, "Stop covering your face with a towel. You only make yourself look ridiculous."

I pulled at the towel to uncover one eye and looked up at him but said nothing. I badly needed to get some sleep and I couldn't care less if I looked ridiculous. I wondered what he would do if I kept my face covered. He moved on.

The next morning, after breakfast, we were briefed on how to deal with our employers and their various expectations. We received literature about cultural differences between them and us, various tips on housekeeping and how to get along with our foreign families. We were reminded that in Singapore, nobody, not even the Prime Minister, ever wore his shoes inside a house. Everybody went barefooted. The pep talks were actually quite enjoyable. Like the biblical Daniel, I felt at least reassured before being thrown into the lion's den.

By Sunday, which was pick-up day, we finally met our employers. We were dressed in a light blue maid's uniform. The dress had a white collar and came with a white apron, both bordered with lace. The agency had sold us the uniforms back in the Philippines. Mine was one size too big, and I thought I looked old and shabby in it, but I wore it anyway. I could only hope that I would not be required to wear it for the rest of my days in Singapore. During the late evening, my employers, Mr Michael Aw, his wife Chin Kwang, with their two boys, Marc and Kenny, picked me up from the Humana apartment. The couple greeted me in a kind and friendly manner.

Mrs Aw was a slim, good looking woman, 35, who dressed well and carried herself with elegance. I admired her sense of fashion, so much so that I would try to copy her style of dressing in the future. I never achieved the same result. She had a cheerful disposition, with brown eyes that always twinkled with good humour. Mrs Aw was her family's oldest child and a teacher at St. Andrews Junior School. For the next three years, I would call her Mumsy, and she would prove to be one of the best employers I've had — one who communicated well and always dealt with family emergencies calmly and with optimism.

Mr Aw, or Bossy, on the other hand, was about 40, slightly overweight, with thinning hair and thick eyeglasses. He ran his father's home appliances business. He had a great sense of humour, and a somewhat quick temper, and had been known to yell at everybody within earshot in Cantonese when stressed. But true to his good humour, he would soon calm down and everything would be alright again. He never held grudges, was hardworking, and totally devoted to the family. Before Ah Heng, Mumsy's youngest sister, got her own car, Bossy was the family's designated driver during outings.

Marc was five and Kenny was three at the time of my arrival. Marc was a sociable, bright kid who loved tagging alongside his mother as she pursued her various activities. Kenny was three, an independent, intense, thumb-sucking, temperamental little firebrand. He hated losing at games and would get easily annoyed, but he could be very loving and cuddly when he wanted to be.

According to the family, Kenny was responsible for getting me my first overseas job. Humana, it seemed, had sent Mrs Aw several resumés with accompanying photographs. I made it to the family shortlist, but Grandma did not like my picture. She thought I looked fierce. (Fierce, I later discovered, was a Singaporean's way of describing a cranky person.) But Kenny picked me out and that was how I ended up working for them. Till this day, I commend that little boy for having shown impeccable good taste at such an early age.

Upon our arrival at the Aw's Eunos Crescent apartment, I was shown my room and told to rest, as it was already late. My bedroom was large but sparsely furnished, with shaggy, wall-to-wall golden-brown carpeting. The whole room had built-in, padded, wrapped around benches covered with the same material. I suspected it used to be the playroom before my arrival. There were huge windows facing south, with my bed sitting low on the floor. After setting my luggage down, I mentally planted my stakes in the middle of the room. This would be my home, I told myself, for better or worse, for as long as I'm here. Then I changed into a pair of shorts and a t-shirt and went to bed. In the morning, when Mrs Aw knocked at the door, I told her I'll change into my uniform and be out in a minute.

"Just wear your shorts," she said, "We are a very modern Chinese family." She spoke perfect English, with little accent. I was so relieved! From that moment on, Mrs Aw had my complete and unadulterated devotion. I addressed her as Ma'am, the way we had been instructed to do, and I called her that for a few months thereafter. After that, she became Mumsy. I couldn't remember when that exactly started.

After breakfast that first morning, I had the chance to look around the house. It was a three-bedroom HDB flat. The two other bedrooms were the master bedroom, and a smaller one shared by Marc and Kenny. The spacious living room led directly to the dining room, which led to the kitchen/laundry room and to my own bathroom. The walls were papered with warm, cream-coloured material. The whole house had a minimalist yet elegant feel, which I loved. It had big windows all around and consequently, let a lot of sunshine in.

We then went over to spend the whole day at Grandma and Grandpa Han's place — Mumsy's parents — whose house was situated along East Coast Road, in Katong. I was to work there everyday until I have mastered Singaporean cooking under Grandma's tutelage.

That same evening, I met most of Mumsy's family members. These were the people I was going to live with and work for over the next three years. In time, I would feel comfortable enough around them to believe that I was an accepted addition to the family. For now, they all seemed to me a highly educated, gainfully employed, quiet bunch of people who had all their ducks in a row, and I felt small and insignificant beside them.

Grandpa Han was a businessman who ran a big clothing import company. Grandma stayed home to look after the family.

Both grandparents were living with their newly married older son, Kwang, and his wife Bee Leng, as well as Mumsy's two younger sisters, Twee Leng and Twee Heng. These last two were fondly referred to by Grandma as Ah Leng and Ah Heng. The youngest member of the family, Loke Kwang, also known as Ah Chai, was still studying architecture in Australia at the time.

I was impressed by the simplicity of the family's lifestyle. Every one of them except Grandma and Ah Chai had good, well-paying jobs, but everyone took the bus to work. Nobody owned a car except Kwang. Least of all Grandpa, who, according to Mumsy, could afford to drive a Mercedes if he had wanted to, but chose instead to commute by public transport.

Kwang worked at the Ministry of Communications dealing with transport issues while Bee Leng was employed as a public relations consultant at Burson Marsteller.

Having observed the family, I was very impressed with every one of them, especially with Kwang. It was a first impression that stayed with me. Indeed, my opinion of him only improved over the years. I was told that an eldest son occupied a very special place in the Chinese family hierarchy. I've met people like them back in the Philippines. Kwang was one of these special individuals. The difference was that he showed no signs of being a spoiled brat. Kwang displayed no arrogance. He was a quiet person who always treated his parents with great respect. Here was a guy who rarely spoke but listened a lot, his silence one that belied a great intelligence. When he did say something, it was usually short and to the point, or a witty comment on the subject at hand. Trained as a mechanical engineer but working as a communications executive with the government, he has had, on many occasions, to address the people's questions regarding the mechanics of road use. This he did through replies in the newspaper.

Being an aspiring writer, I read Kwang's work with great interest. After my cousin Santa started working for them, she used to collect and show me things Kwang had written for his office newsletter. We both enjoyed reading them. I felt then that Kwang, engineer or not, had a definite future in journalism. In the meantime, I heard he was doing a really good job in the Civil Service. Mumsy said the government liked employing engineers because such people were trained to look at things objectively and analytically, and they were the best kind of workers. Kwang became my secret role model. I called him *Da Hotshot*.

Bee Leng was the Super Mom, very smart, very capable, and with a no-nonsense attitude. She spoke her mind frankly but in a non-abrasive manner. She looked after her husband and their home with flawless efficiency. In time, I would find out that behind Bee Leng's straight-talking exterior was hidden a sensitive and extremely compassionate nature. Bee Leng spoke and read French fluently, along with several Chinese dialects.

Ah Leng and Ah Heng — The Girls — were Mumsy's two younger sisters. Heng and I were of the same age, but that was where the similarity ended. I called Ah Heng Hotshot No. 2. Heng was an advertising executive with Singapore Airlines, while Leng worked as a secretary in a business office downtown. Both girls were classy dressers, feminine and well educated, nothing like the loud country bumpkin that I was. Neither Leng nor Heng talked very much, and during my training days, they would sit for a while with Mumsy and the kids after work, then retire early to their bedroom to read after dinner. Nobody watched television except Grandpa and the boys.

I enjoyed going to Grandma's everyday. I loved East Coast Road. It was an old-style street with trees growing along its sidewalks, with old buildings that didn't go higher than four storeys. There were coffee shops and itinerant food vendors that could be found all along the road.

We could get snacks like *rojak, mee goreng, yong tau foo* and *pisang goreng* from street vendors any time of the day. Sometimes, Mumsy would send me down to buy something from these vendors. I liked watching them and their little food carts because they reminded me of the Philippine's own sidewalk sellers.

Slowly but surely, I learned to live with a Singaporean family, absorbing information about their food and culture by osmosis. I gained an even better understanding of the country and the ways of its people through reading. At the time of my arrival, there were about 5,000 Filipino domestic workers in Singapore, along with thousands more from Malaysia, Sri Lanka, and a few from Thailand.

Before domestic workers from other countries were legally allowed into Singapore in 1978, families here used to employ local amahs. Amahs were usually local single women who work as hired help, mainly looking after the children and doing housekeeping. This breed of domestics started dying off as locals became more affluent. With the new economic boom in Singapore, which saw many Singaporean wives enter the workforce, families now find it necessary to look for domestic help outside of the country, to keep an eye on the children. The government thus saw fit to relax immigration rules for foreign domestic workers. At the time of my arrival, in 1984, Singapore was already a dynamic, vibrant city. The whole place was clean and green, and efficiency was its middle name. Humana was doing brisk business, having established a reputation for bringing in well-trained maids.

The Prime Minister of the country at the time was Mr Lee Kuan Yew, a visionary by reputation, and the man who authored the independence and prosperity that Singapore had been enjoying for years. After having compared the Philippines and its recent history to Singapore's, I felt a huge amount of envy. Prime Minister Lee has proven that size didn't matter. It's not how big the club, but how you wield it. Singapore is merely a dot on the world map, but look how loud it bleeps on the world's economic radar screen.

I thought about every rebel faction that wanted to cut its ties with the Philippines. I recalled thinking, were I to ever become President, I'd tell those guys, "Go ahead, pick your island." The Philippines has about 7,100 islands and at least half a dozen of these are bigger than Singapore. There should be enough to go around. I'm sure we could manage to turn at least one island into a prosperous, clean and peaceful place like Singapore!

CLOSE ENCOUNTERS

I landed in Singapore with my sleeves rolled up, ready to work as a domestic help. By my own deluded standards, I was an excellent housekeeper. Although my employers and I hadn't really sat down together to establish ground rules, I was sure I could handle anything. *Veni vidi vici* — or so I had felt.

I was soon to find out that there were aspects to domestic work that I wasn't prepared for. Here were some of them:

LANGUAGE

Firstly, there was the language barrier. Everyone in the family, including the children, spoke excellent English, especially Mumsy. I had no problem understanding Mumsy and the boys. But my Sir, or Bossy, was a different matter altogether. Although he spoke several languages, I found his diction hard to understand. He had a heavy Singlish accent, and he spoke very fast. I had to ask him to repeat whatever he said at least three times. This he did patiently, and I realised later how much restraint he had to muster to get me to understand him.

For example, he would call home to ask if his wife had phoned. He'd say, "Ma'am rang up?"

It all sounded gobbledygook to me, so I asked, "What?" I hadn't yet mastered the more polite way of asking, "Pardon me?"

He'd then repeat the question again, now slower. I still didn't get it. So he'd repeat it several times over, until an electric bulb lit up inside my head. "Oh-h-h. Oh no, Sir, Ma'am didn't call."

Then there was Grandma Han, whose job it was to teach me cooking. We had one little problem. Grandma spoke only Hainanese, with sprinklings of Malay, English and other Chinese dialects. I spoke English. We started communicating by sign language, augmented by the few English words we knew in common. The end result was a wholly new language, spoken only by Grandma and myself, to the surprise and amusement of the entire family.

TECHNOLOGY

I had my first run-in with Bossy on my second day on the job, after coming home from Grandma's. This experience taught me a lot about myself. I might believe I was domesticated, but there were certain things I still had to learn, like controlling my temper.

We arrived home from Grandma's after a heavy downpour. The kitchen windows had been left partially open and small puddles of rainwater had formed on the floor. Unbeknownst to Bossy and me, other things had also been drenched. We were both standing in the kitchen when Bossy reached up to the light switch and flicked it on.

"Oww!" he howled. It seemed some water had seeped into the switch and Bossy had a nasty little electric shock. Jumping away from the switch, Bossy asked me to hand him a kitchen towel.

So I did.

The cloth I handed him was damp, and he received another jolt. He dropped the towel and jumped again, now in disgust. The whole event seemed so funny that I started laughing.

Bossy glared at me and yelled, "This is not funny. Electricity here is different from electricity in the Philippines!" I didn't think his shouting was funny either. Feeling offended, I screamed back, "Electricity is the same here and in the Philippines. Different how? Pray tell me!"

Bossy was shocked into silence. Never did he expect to be spoken to like that, by a two-day-old maid, no less. On my part, I was so angry I marched straight into my room and banged the door shut.

It did not cross my mind then that I could be fired and sent back to the Philippines in disgrace first thing the next morning.

Fortunately for me, Mumsy was kind and understanding. Being a schoolteacher, she possessed skills to handle a crisis just like this. She knocked on my door a few minutes later, to find out why I shouted at

Sir before stomping into my room. I told her we had a disagreement regarding electrical matters, and by the way, he shouted first. I walked out because he couldn't explain his point.

She laughed, then said, "Don't pay attention to his outbursts. Sir's bark is worse than his bite." I thanked her and told her I was sorry. I had calmed down by this time and had regained my senses. I was ready to throw myself on the ground and kiss the hem of her skirt.

What happened on that second day set the tone of my relationship with the Aw family. This wouldn't be my last disagreement with the boss, and Mumsy would always be there to smooth things out between us. And Bossy, despite his gruff manners, was actually a good-hearted person. The fact that Bossy and I both love and respect Mumsy helped maintain peace in the house.

On my third day, I singed my eyelashes.

To get the water heater to work, you had to light up a little gas furnace, but you had to time it perfectly. First, Mumsy would run a bit of the water in the bathroom, then she would call out, "OK, light it up!" When I called back that it's lighted, she'd turned the water on full stream and start the bath. At least in theory, that's how it was supposed to work.

So I climbed up on a chair and turned the lighter on. I called out OK, not noticing that the lighter failed to work. By this time, Mumsy had started running her bath. I lighted the furnace again. In a flash, the gaseous build-up around the lighter exploded in my face, singeing my eyelashes and eyebrows. I fell off the chair and hit the floor with a loud thud. Mumsy came running into the kitchen to help me up, before showing me how to do it properly. Not long after that, Mumsy got us an electric water heater.

DISCIPLINE

My Singaporean family believed in the old biblical saying: Spare the rod and spoil the child. We kept several canes all over the house in support of this belief. These canes were thin, about two-foot in length, and made of rattan. Installation consisted of hanging the cane to a nail on the wall, which was done strategically, so that the kids could see the canes, but not get them down. These disciplinary weapons could easily be bought at the market for 25 cents each.

I loved canes. It was my sceptre of authority, although I never had to use the cane on the boys, and neither did their parents. The mere thought of getting a whipping kept the children well behaved.

When mayhem threatened, I would make a big show of climbing up on a chair to get the cane down, brandish it around, make whizzing sounds in the air with it, and they'd fall back in line in a hurry.

There were days when I badly needed a cane to re-assert my alpha position over the kids — not an easy thing if you're 4"10 (1.47m) and barely taller than them — but I won't be able to find one. So I would announce loudly, "Marc Aw-ah, I know where you're hiding those canes, so bring them out, or else, there will be trouble." Canes would be produced from under beds or cupboards immediately.

Being devoted Christians, my employers also believed in loving your enemies. The general idea was, if someone slapped you on one cheek, you should offer him the other as well. From where I come from — a province known for its machismo — if you slapped someone, you could end up looking down the barrel of a .45. At the very least, you got slapped back. So when Marc returned home from school sobbing one day, and reported that his best friend had hit him, I immediately replied, "Hit him back. He can't be your friend if he's hurting you."

I said this within earshot of Mumsy, who was horrified by my advice. "You're clever to teach, hah, remember what the bible says..." A biblical discussion would then follow.

GARBAGE DISPOSAL

In my mind, one of the marvels of Singapore housekeeping was its efficient rubbish disposal system.

We lived in a 20-storey building in Eunos Crescent. Our apartment was on the 14th floor. Initially, I wondered how we dealt with the garbage, and feared that it was going to be my job to haul the trash all the way down each night. That worry never materialised. I soon discovered that every apartment building had several collection bins, and each unit had a little access vent on a wall in the kitchen, covered by a flip-top metallic lid. All you had to do was drop your trash through the chute, which would then fall smack into the huge collection bin waiting at ground level. These bins would be emptied daily by contracted garbage collectors.

I gained intimate knowledge of the workings of this chute through an experience I recorded in my journal under the title, *Close Encounters of the Smelly Kind.*

One day, Mumsy accidentally left her identity card hidden under some used paper napkins on the dining table. Unsuspectingly, I walked into the kitchen and, seeing the table in a mess, swept everything into a plastic bag, then knotted it and threw it down the chute.

A Singaporean's identity card is an important piece of document that every citizen is required to carry with them. If you lose your card, you're required to get a new one, after paying a replacement fee of about S$50.

Mumsy realised she lost her card some minutes after leaving the dining room. She swore she left it on the dinner table, while I firmly maintained I never saw it. She believed me and we frantically looked for it all over the house. Ultimately, I had to go down and search for it in THE BIN, just to be sure.

My habit of knotting up the plastic bags before disposal saved my butt that day. I climbed into the huge container and started rooting around for the plastic bag I junked just half an hour ago. I couldn't see it anywhere, so I dug deeper through the trash, while banana peels, gooey left-overs, used diapers, and various items of refuse clung close to me. I was almost in tears when I spotted my bag under a foot-deep of debris. I dragged it away from the rubbish bin and rummaged through it. *Voila!* The identity card WAS indeed in the bag.

Since that day, I never let anything pass through the chute without first giving it a thorough once-over.

LAUNDRY

Every foreign visitor to the country will be impressed by the colourful flags of clothes drying in the sun, outside high-rise apartments. It's laundry, Singapore style. Pieces of clothing were first clipped onto bamboo poles, which were then placed in neat rows in specially constructed holders outside kitchen windows.

On sunny days, the kitchen side of every apartment building in Eunos Crescent would be draped in a symphony of colours, with clothes waving, dancing, fluttering in the breeze. Drying laundry this way was very effective and economical, as compared to using an electric dryer.

I am a small person, but I am quite strong, so I didn't mind hanging out the laundry. Once I mastered the art of placing a loaded seven-foot bamboo pole into its holder outside, I was fairly happy.

Here's how I do it: First, I clip the laundry onto the pole, then open the window grill with one hand, and climb up on a chair while carrying the pole with the other hand. I would then wrap one leg around the middle window beam; keep the other leg/foot firmly planted on the chair, and carefully fit the pole into its holder, while making sure the whole contraption stayed balanced. There you go. Easy.

While doing all this, however, my upper body would be sticking out of the window. One wrong move and my pole and its load would be plummeting 14 floors like an errant javelin. When that happened, the laundry would have to be redone, then the whole process would be repeated.

I never considered the possibility that I could go down with my laundry, leaving my employers with the unpleasant task of scraping my remains off the pavement below, and sending it back to the Philippines in a sealed body bag.

A year later, someone pointed this out to me.

A Church friend, Arlin, a Filipino engineer working as a construction site foreman here, was flabbergasted when he saw how I hung out the laundry one day, when I invited him and several friends over for lunch. The following Sunday, Arlin brought me a safety belt, a regulation accessory for everyone working on tall buildings. I was to buckle one end to the window beam and secure my waist with the other. I tried the belt once but found that it slowed me down considerably, so I did not use it again.

What if I did fall out of that window wearing the safety belt? I would then be flailing around at the end of the belt while trying to regain my foothold on the window's ledge. That vision seemed less romantic to me than actually falling to my death. Anyway, the fact that I'm still around today was proof that my own technique wasn't as dangerous as it looked.

GRANDMA AND ME

My adventures in Singapore started on my first day of work. Mumsy gave me an alarm clock, a dark orange timepiece with big green digital numbers and a wake up call that reminded me of the sound trains make when approaching a station. Mumsy said she got it as a wedding present. The first morning the alarm sounded, I was so startled I must have bounced a few inches high. I've never used alarm clocks before.

Everyday during my training period, Marc and Kenny, Mumsy and I would get up early and go off to Grandma's. It was the school holidays so everybody was home. After breakfast, we would get our things ready and Bossy would drive us down to Grandma's on his way to work. Mumsy would stay around with us most of the time, unless she had something to do at school.

Grandma Han was my first and very best friend in Singapore. Mumsy served as our chief interpreter when she was around. In her absence, when things couldn't be expressed through hand signals, we enlisted the help of Marc Aw, five years old, who was only too happy to help. The kid, however, could get so muddled doing translations back and forth that he would end up speaking English to Grandma and Hainanese to me. We did this until Grandma and I had evolved our very own language, one that served us so well we could actually talk about current events, gossip a little bit, and discuss our cooking plans.

Mumsy told me that when I first arrived, Grandma was impressed that I didn't look at all flashy. This was understandable. I wore no jewellery because I never liked wearing them, aside from the fact that I had sold whatever pieces I used to own. My nails weren't painted. I hated painting them. I had no make-up; never used any. I wore shorts and t-shirt everyday, a habit formed in childhood when I realised that climbing trees were easier if you don't wear dresses. Also, it was easier to keep up with four big brothers who did not want a wimpy, dressed-up little sister following them around. I would have gone to church in shorts and t-shirt if I could get away with it.

Added to that was my utter lack of interest in talking on the phone or in looking for friends. During my learning period, my Singaporean family was company enough. So Grandma phoned her friends and told them about me. Her friends — them of little faith — responded, "She can't be much different from all the others. Once she starts going out with other maids, she'll show her true colours. Just you wait a few weeks." Grandma eventually proved them wrong, and I was pleased that unknowingly, even after I had acquired new friends, I did not let her down.

My first task upon arrival at Grandma's was housecleaning. I dusted every inch of the house, crawled after cobwebs under beds, mopped the floor, and cleaned the kitchen counters. I did this every time we went to her house. No corner of the house was safe from my scrubbing, unless Grandma told me otherwise.

During my first few weeks, I was so unused to continuous physical work that by the end of two hours, my back would hurt, my knees would shake and I would feel really hungry. Grandma always sensed this and she'd give me a snack, which I would gratefully accept.

After lunch, I would clear the kitchen and wash the kitchen floor, and then, I would have some time for rest. Grandma didn't mind me sneaking a nap on a row of dining room chairs in the mid-afternoons. My real job started before dinnertime.

Actually, Grandma and I did not need a lot of words to understand each other. She would move towards the kitchen and off I went after her. I shadowed Grandma around whenever she started dinner. I had a small notebook where I wrote everything she did, like the way carrots were cut, how shallots and chillies were prepared, and how everything was seasoned and spiced up; the precise timing when every item hit the wok and when they were taken out.

Under Grandma's supervision, I learned to prepare family favourites like Hainanese chicken rice, chilli prawns, Hokkien mee, steamed fish; meat, seafood and vegetable curries, *poh piah*, and the different soups we had with dinner. We spent many hours together, chopping, dicing, slicing, pounding spices, wrapping spring rolls in comfortable silence.

One of the skills I tried to master was the cutting up of a whole cooked chicken into serving pieces. I observed Grandma countless times as she positioned the whole boiled chicken on a wooden cutting board placed over a bunch of clean newspapers on the floor, and noted how, with precise movements, she would hold a leg with her left hand and proceed to cut the subject into clean little pieces. No chicken part ever flew off the cutting board and ended on the newspaper. After cutting, she would arrange the chicken beautifully and neatly on a serving platter.

Remembering my own miserable efforts to duplicate her technique, I could only assume that it must have been painful for Grandma to watch me.

Grandma always made sure that our meals were balanced and well-prepared. Daily fare consisted of vegetables, meat or seafood or both, rice and soup, and the ever-present Singaporean all-time popular dip, chopped *chilli padi* in light soy sauce. Variations of this dip could include *cincalok*, or salted shrimps, and chopped shallots.

Grandma's kitchen, like everyone else's in Singapore, had multi-racial spices in its cupboards — Indian, Malay, Chinese and others. I learned that food was classified into two types — heaty and cooling — according to their effect on a person's body. Consuming a combination of food that kept the *yin* and the *yang* of the body in perfect balance resulted in good health.

For instance, oranges were considered heaty, so if you had a cough, you shouldn't eat oranges because then, your coughing could get worse. If you were having a cold, it followed that eating warming food and soups would help you get better. Examples of cooling things were drinks like barley water with rock sugar, or boiled dried berries with roots and sugar cane sticks. We always kept a jug of those in Grandma's fridge.

I loved Grandma's soups — made with dried herbs, dried berries or lotus roots, simmered for hours with pork or mutton, then topped with fresh watercress, winter gourd, or other vegetables. They were always tasty and refreshing. Grandma's soups were some of the things I missed most when I went away from Singapore.

I have tried to cook the same recipes since, but I never enjoyed them as much as I used to. I have concluded that pleasure in eating depended as much on the company as the flavour of the food being shared.

Grandma and I would prepare everything for dinner, but we kept them uncooked until a few minutes before meal time. The family always ate things steaming hot. We never used microwave ovens back then. Those being new technology, both Mumsy and I distrusted them.

After dinner preparations and before the adults had dinner, I would feed the children while they watched T.V. Marc Aw was five and Kenny three, but I still fed them, up to the time Marc entered Primary One. I had to do it because, amazingly, these children were totally disinterested in food.

When I was a kid, I ate without being fed, and so did my children after me. The difference, I guess, laid in the fact that they had so much, while we barely had enough. These boys had to be fed spoonful-by-spoonful, until they stopped opening their mouths, which meant they had had enough.

Kenny was a more efficient eater. Marc was harder to feed because he didn't swallow his food right away. He kept his food in his mouth until his cheeks bulged, and I had to prod his cheek so he would swallow. It didn't work all the time. Sometimes, the bulge merely got bigger in the other cheek.

We did this for a year until I gave up. I thought if he had to feed himself, he would pay more attention.

I discussed this with Bossy, and told him, "The boy is six years old.

How long are we going to do this? I think it's time he feeds himself."
No problem. Bossy turned to Marc and ordered, "Marc Aw-ah, feed
yourself."

After that, the boys ate by themselves while watching TV and I
spent more time with Grandma in the kitchen.

I usually set the table. The family always ate dinner together,
including myself. We would sit around a huge dinner table, with the
various dishes set up on a revolving lazy Susan, and everyone would
drink soup from a big common bowl. I felt very privileged sharing a
meal with them this way.

It did take me months to develop a taste for spicy food though. I
used to eat everything without complaining, even as I felt the inside
of my cheeks burn and my tongue turn numb. Numbness was good,
because after that, I could eat whatever was being served.

One day, I suddenly realised that I could now taste my food.
Everyone watched in awe as I filled my plate with curry gravy until
my rice was almost swimming in it. I took a bite of the chopped chilli
and crushed it between my teeth, and reveled in the heat that seared
my mouth. The secret was to never let the chilli seeds touch your lip,
as it could really hurt, like having accidentally taken a sip of scalding
coffee.

Several months later, my training was declared over, and I was
Grandma-certified, meaning I was now deemed to have qualified as a
home chef.

This being the case, we went back to Eunos Crescent to live our own
lives and joined Grandma and the rest of the family only on Saturday
nights for dinner. Grandma and I remained close, however, and I
always looked forward to helping out at Grandma's kitchen.

Three years after my arrival, Grandma passed away, at the age of 64.
She had a heart attack.

Nobody was prepared for it. Grandpa had just gone into retirement
and had made many happy plans for Grandma and himself. He would

take her on holidays abroad. Grandma deserved it. She had worked devotedly at home and raised a family for 39 years. Now, all the children were grown up. Two of them were married and already have families of their own.

But Grandma's heart failed her. It failed all of us.

There was nothing we could do about it. After the funeral, when we came back to the house that was still filled with her presence, I looked at her large photograph, and thoughts of Grandma started crowding my brain.

I knew I was going to miss her.

Grandma was a skilled housekeeper, a loving Mum, a doting grandmother, a patient teacher. It wasn't what I had expected at all. Other maids from my agency had warned me about grandmothers — those malevolent, elderly women who were the curse of foreign domestics.

They breathed down your neck the whole time, watched you like a hawk, and took great pleasure in finding dust where you least suspected it, pointing out spots of dirt you have missed with vicious glee. They were known to be very strict and they required every ounce of your energy at all times.

My Grandma turned out to be different, and I immediately fell in love with her. Grandma didn't command or instruct, but quietly set an example of cleanliness, speed and efficiency for me to follow. It was an unspoken challenge she offered, and which I accepted.

Grandma's patience was legendary. All she did was groan "*aiyohhh!*" when I chipped the ear of her favourite porcelain tea kettle, or broke one of her dinner plates, or threw her strainer down the rubbish chute by accident.

Grandma was always cheerful, and generous. She would often give me things she knew I'd appreciate and watch with pleasure the joy with which I received them.

Grandma used the different special occasions throughout the year as an excuse to buy me clothes. I always get red packets from Grandma during Chinese New Year.

I left Singapore for Vancouver a few months after Grandma passed away, but I still cry each time I think about her.

I still miss her, even today.

She wasn't just Grandma by name. To me, she was my Grandma — friend, mentor, and family.

THE EUNOS FAMILY

After Grandma had given me the nod for my culinary skills, I moved permanently back to my boss' apartment at Eunos Crescent. Down there, life followed a loose routine.

Every school morning, my alarm clock would trumpet at 6 am and I would stagger to the kitchen. I made coffee, then prepared a slice of toast and a soft-boiled egg for Marc. I would pour Bossy's and Mumsy's coffee and then wake up the family. Bossy would wake up Marc Aw and help him change into his school uniform. Marc would be half asleep during the whole process, until his Dad deposited him on a chair in front of his soft-boiled egg and toast. He would look at his breakfast, then go right back to sleep, head propped up on his arm, leaving his food untouched.

Mumsy would come out of the bedroom, take a sip of her coffee and hustle the whole group out of the house. Bossy would hoist the sleeping Marc over his shoulder and off they went. I assumed Marc Aw would eventually wake up at some point before reaching St. Andrews Junior School.

I didn't know why I ever bothered with getting them breakfast, because the same thing would happen everyday. Marc Aw never ate anything in the morning. The boss would drink his coffee and run off, and Mumsy would look at her full mug of coffee, before taking one single sip. The woman did not really need a whole mug, I decided. So one morning, I served her half a mug. I heard about it immediately. Mumsy said, "I want more coffee."

I asked, "What for? You never drink it up anyway."

Her reply, "I don't know. I just want my full cup of coffee."

Years later, it came to pass that someone was serving me coffee regularly. I never finished my coffee either. So my friend decreed that half a cup should be okay. I felt deprived right away. Even though I never drank the whole thing, it felt good to see that I was getting my normal share. Less than that didn't seem to taste as good. After a short discussion on the amount of coffee I required each morning, I settled down and silently saluted Mumsy with my coffee mug.

Each morning, Kenny Aw and I were left to do our own thing. This was before he, too, went off to school. The two of us usually went down to the void deck after breakfast to meet and play with Tina and the little boy she was looking after. Like mine, Tina's family had two little boys, who were the same age as Marc and Kenny. This was good because Kenny got to play with someone his own age and I got to hang out with Tina. Sometimes, we went to the Eunos Crescent Hawker Centre to buy back lunch and eat it together at Tina's apartment.

Tina's family spoke Mandarin at home so Tina learned to speak it. She communicated with her boys in Mandarin, first haltingly, then quite fluently. I suspected she even learned a few swear words. How else would her kids be so well behaved with just one firm, dangerous sounding admonition from Tina?

I was very impressed and very jealous. My own family spoke English at home. Bossy talked on the phone, even swore, in several languages, but those times were few and far between. He only addressed Mumsy in Cantonese, his native tongue, whenever they had to discuss touchy matters not meant for the kids' or nanny's ears. Mumsy invariably replied in Hainanese, so I stayed ignorant of whatever was happening.

I was so envious that Tina was learning something new and I wasn't, that I ordered a set of tapes teaching me how to speak and read Mandarin. It cost me a small fortune but I considered it a good investment. Initially, that was. Everyday, after all my chores were done, I would go to my room and listen to the tapes, carefully repeating after each word. I learned to count from one to 10, then my sense of humour took over. Here I was, trying to learn a foreign language by tape, and I sounded funny even to my own ears. I would often end up laughing so hard each time I tried to articulate a difficult sounding word that I had to stop listening. Linguist I wasn't. In the long run, listening enabled me to tell what language everyone was speaking by their phrasing and the sounds they made.

After Kenny started going to school, he and Marc took the school bus together everyday. I was left on my own for most of the day. So after everybody was gone, it was time for me to start my own morning. Nobody came home for lunch on weekdays so I was free to do the household chores until I start preparing for dinner. The first order of the day was breakfast.

I discovered a small store that sold *nasi lemak* and other breakfast fare at the void deck of the building adjacent to ours. *Nasi lemak* became my all time favourite, because it represented to me all the best of Singaporean food. Fried *ikan bilis* and peanuts, on rice cooked in coconut milk, with a side dish of fried, sweet and spicy sambal, washed down by a mug of coffee every morning, and I was ready to rule the world.

After breakfast, I loaded the washing machine and, afterwards, started vacuuming. I loved our vacuum cleaner. It was an old Hoover — loud, round, flat and sat low on the floor, with industrial strength pulling capacity. Nothing was safe from that old hummer if it happened to be within sucking range. On a few occasions, I've had to fight to recover from its bowels portions of Mumsy's bed sheets, or various other family possessions.

For lunch, I would usually go down to the hawker centre to buy take-away food, or steam some rice and seafood at home. My hawker centre favourites included *char siew* rice, chicken rice and *roti prata*. I never ate at the hawker centre by myself but brought my food home. Every time I bought *char siew* rice, the stall owner would try to entice me to leave my employers and work for him instead — with higher pay, he promised. I couldn't tell whether he was serious, but I always told him I wasn't looking for another employer and that I was happy where I was, thank you.

At around three in the afternoon, I would wait at the void deck for the bus that dropped off Marc and Kenny. I would get them upstairs and get them changed, then give them some time for play and rest. I tried to get them to nap, if I could. Afterwards, I would take Marc and Kenny to a tutor who would work with them on mathematics and the Chinese language. Studying and preparing for lessons at home never seemed to be enough. Going to a tutor was a way of life for these young students. Singaporean children seemed to spend an inordinate amount of time studying, in school and out. Every student, like my friend Theresa Devasahayam, seemed driven to excel. It was, and it still is, an academically competitive culture.

After school, homework, and tuition classes, Marc, Kenny and I would play in the house. I can't remember why we chose to stay at home, maybe it was what the children wanted, but we spent our weekday afternoons indoors playing kiddy games or watching TV. This was a time before videos, so we mainly watched cartoons. Or we played in the living room.

We played a lot! The boys had all sorts of toys, and the rule was, the boys were to put their own toys away after every playtime. This was an exercise in learning responsibility. Some days, there seemed to be more clutter than usual. (Children are such perverse creatures. When you're trying to talk to someone, or use the phone, they're immediately beside you, tugging at your sleeves or whining about something, always demanding attention. Let go of the phone and they disappear. When playthings are scattered all over the house, a kid wouldn't touch them. But try tidying them up, and every toy suddenly seemed important, and the whole lot will be taken out 30 seconds after everything was put away.)

Marc and Kenny were no different, but they knew they were expected to clear their toys away after playing with them. If you knew children, you'd realise that this did not always happen automatically. It could take a fair bit of nagging.

Down here, domestic workers are commonly called maids or servants. I did not like being called a servant. I couldn't explain why, except for the fact that in Tagalog, the translation for servant was *alila*, which, in my mind, meant an unpaid worker who worked in exchange for room and board. An *alila* was lower in status compared to a maid, the latter being commonly referred to back home as *katulong* or helper; a professional domestic. It was splitting hairs, I knew, but it was very important to me to be called a maid and not a servant. Go figure.

One day, when I was still new at the job, I told Kenny Aw to put away his toys after he had finished playing with them. Kenny, three years old, replied, "You're the servant, you put them away." I sat him down and told him I was not a servant. Then, I reported this to Mumsy, who agreed, and told Kenny, "Crisanta is your friend, not your servant, OK?" I felt somewhat petty and embarrassed afterwards, because now it seemed such a trivial matter. The more I thought about the incident, the more I realised that being called a maid or a servant made no difference. No big deal. They were just words. What really mattered was how the family treated you.

Mumsy took over the care of the boys after she arrived home from school, to give me time to prepare dinner. After the evening meal, the boys would go back to their homework, while I did the dishes. Mumsy might watch TV after dinner. Invariably, she would get hungry around eight or nine o'clock. What did you expect? We had dinner at six o'clock and she would hardly eat anything. So she'd be thinking about food. Usually. it was *oh luak*, *char kuay teow*, or *mee siam*. Who would be going out to find her favourite snacks but Bossy? He would be only too happy to get his wife whatever she wanted.

One of the things I liked about Bossy was he usually treated Mumsy like a princess, even during days when they were having their spats. At times of discord, I was, of course, staunchly on Mumsy's side. When, for one reason or another — always his fault, I was thinking, by the way — they would get into some heated, multi-lingual exchange of words, and he started losing his temper, Bossy found it prudent to leave the house to cool off. I supposed he knew that going against one very displeased wife and one very disapproving maid standing behind her was a losing battle.

One aspect of housework I wasn't too excited about was doing the laundry. This was one skill my aunt never taught me, because a cousin got the job when we were kids. I never learned to wash clothes in the village either, because either my mother or my big sister would do it. Doing the laundry in Singapore was all right because we had a washing machine. I used to put everything in the machine, pre-sorted into whites and coloreds, of course, including the kids' sneakers. The shoes being laundered would be going *thump, thump, thump*, which worried me a bit, but they would come out clean and wrung, and I did not even have to use a laundry brush. The intricacies of hanging them out to dry you've heard about. The only pieces of clothing I had to wash by hand were Mumsy's silk outfits. Since I wasn't too enamoured of washing clothes, you wouldn't be surprised about my feelings regarding ironing.

I loathed ironing! As a kid before the advent of the electric iron, I had watched my big sister struggle with a charcoal-fed, flat iron, those smoky gadgets you had to fill with charcoal and then fan to get the embers and the heat going. It was a very interesting activity, but only if you're watching the whole process from the sidelines. Thank God electricity had arrived by the time I was required to do ironing. In Mumsy's house, we had a deep, woven bamboo basket where I kept the clothes waiting to be ironed. Mainly in the basket were Bossy's office clothes and the basket was always half-full. I ironed as much as I could everyday, but I was a slow ironer. I only learned to do it properly in Singapore.

So I would iron some of Bossy's clothes each day, starting with the ones that had been in the basket longest, just to keep him happy and clothed. I laundered and ironed the boys' uniforms too. It seemed to me that Bossy always got the short end of the stick, laundry-wise. Sometimes, he would be chasing after a favourite shirt and guess where it would be? I would then pull it out from under a big pile of clothes and hurriedly get it onto the ironing board. Obviously, my system for handling Bossy's laundry didn't work very well. Whenever I recall these infractions today, I shake my head in wonder. How the heck did I get away with *that*?

My culinary skills improved considerably after a year in Singapore. I even loved making chilli and *belachan* sauces from scratch.

However, while I enjoyed cooking, I remained a bad meal planner. My creativity did not extend to thinking up new dishes or even experimenting from the cookbooks that Mumsy collected when we started eating at home. Left to my own devices, I would be cooking the same recipes day after day. I never did Western or Filipino dishes as I never learned how to prepare those. Mumsy, on the other hand, loved trying out new dishes. She would plan the menu whenever she had time. That worked very well for both of us. She planned and I executed. Between Mumsy and me, our culinary repertoire grew and my cooking got even better, so much better that Bossy jokingly said once that I could now be rented out as a cook.

On Saturday evenings, we all went to Grandma's for dinner. The rest of the family would be there too, including Kwang and Bee Leng, their baby, Ming Chou, and their maid, my cousin Santa. Whenever we visited the East Coast Road home, Grandma was still chief cook and I was still her sous chef. Bossy still exclusively and regularly did the chilli crabs. Sometimes, dinner would be at Eunos Crescent, in which case either Bossy or I would cook. If it was chilli crab time, Bossy would bring home a bunch of live crabs — the fresher the better the flavour. I was once again relegated to the role of assistant cook, but I didn't mind, except when Bossy asked me to kill the crabs. This I refused to do.

Killing crabs by stabbing them with a chopstick between the eyes wasn't exactly my favourite gig. I always left that task to Bossy, but I was happy to wash and clean the crabs afterwards. This repulsion to killing things dated back to my pre-school days in the farm, when we had a multitude of animals — chickens, goats, pigs, cows, cats and dogs.

That was a time when I named every animal and played with it, because I was all by myself while my older siblings did their grown-up things. Imagine my horror each time I saw one of my former playmates on the dinner table, pieces floating in broth or skewered with bamboo sticks and ready for consumption. It was enough to drive me to vegetarianism in my childhood days. It got so bad that every time my mother was butchering or selling one of the farm animals, I had to be sent out to the neighbours for the day. I did not believe in eating my friends; however, this belief was not shared by the rest of my barbaric family. To them, a chicken, pig or dog ceased being a "friend" if it was served up as food. It was something I just couldn't reconcile with. Of course, as with everything else, there was an exception. I didn't mind eating chicken — or any other animal I hadn't formed any friendship with.

When we didn't cook, we would eat out. Bossy knew all the best hawker centres around town; where to get the best eats and the best drinks. Hokkien mee and *poh piah* from Newton Circus, curry puffs from Serangoon, *rojak* from a particular coffee shop in Katong, *nyonya kuey* from Bengawan Solo. On special occasions, the whole extended family, which included Kwang and Bee Leng after they moved into their own house in Serangoon Gardens, would go to one of the big restaurants in the city, or to seafood eateries in Punggol.

Eating out was a lot of fun, although according to Bossy, Mumsy and I ate like birds. We'd peck at our food. So Mumsy and I sometimes shared an order when we ate out. Everybody ate with obvious appetite, except Mumsy, who would be tossing her Hokkien Mee or *mee siam* around with her chopsticks. The food didn't seem to be getting consumed or anything. So I'd ask, "Your food is still on your plate. What are you actually eating?"

She'd look at me with laughter in her eyes. "Air."

In Singapore, when eating out, I don't remember ever bringing leftover food back. We never kept leftovers at home either. It was unheard of, something I assumed every family did. After every meal, I'd ask Mumsy what I should do about the uneaten portions. She would motion towards the rubbish chute and drone, "Throw away. Throw away."

My friends and I marveled at this many times, as we talked about all the other starving people in the world. I wished there was a way to send all these leftovers to the under-nourished people in the Philippines, or in Africa. Back home, we never throw away leftovers. There was always room for it in the next meal, or it became dog food.

Bossy, on the other hand, loved his food. I used to jokingly call him our "finishing department". He had enough appetite to stand in for the whole family. When I was feeling nasty, I told him he also ate like a bird, then gloated snidely to myself, "A vulture. Har har!"

Bossy was a great guy, make no mistake about it, but we seemed to be locked together in some sort of endless bickering, an odd relationship that started on my second day in Singapore. Call it a personality conflict. He had no problems drawing out the Bitch in me.

Let me illustrate: One Sunday, I attended church with the family. After the service, Mumsy was engaged in some lighthearted conversation with Auntie Soh Hian, her best friend. Marc and Kenny were chasing each other in and around the rows of chairs. There was nothing much for me to do, so I sat down to read my bible, while watching the boys from the corner of my eye.

Along came Bossy to remind me I was slacking. He commented, "You're supposed to look after them, you know." Of course, he was totally within his rights in telling me this.

But the Bitch snapped the bible shut and stood up without much encouragement from the rest of me, and replied with un-Christian sarcasm, "What d'ya want me to do, carry them around?"

"Whoa," he said. "This maid very fierce, *lah*."

Probably feeling gracious after a morning of prayers, Bossy let that one pass. His kindness showed in his actions. I remember locking myself out of the house one day. I had hurriedly run out of the apartment with the children to catch the school bus, and had forgotten my keys. I usually had them in my shorts pocket, but it must have fallen out the night before. After realising I was locked out, I went over to my friend Tina's place to page for Bossy. He responded immediately, driving all the way from Jurong to Eunos Crescent. He could have given me a big sermon that time, but he didn't. Jurong, I think, is about 20 minutes' drive from Eunos Crescent.

Weekends were different. On Saturday mornings, we got to hang around the house longer, before everybody rushed out the door and went somewhere. Bossy usually went out to get breakfast. After that, he would go to work, while Mumsy would go to school. She often took Marc with her. Kenny, on the other hand, didn't mind staying home and playing with me.

On occasions, when both boys had to be left at home with me, things always followed a set pattern. Marc would raise a big racket; Kenny and I would leave him alone; he would sulk, then calm down, and finally, he would decide to join us in our games. After he got used to staying behind with us, there was less trouble. The boys watched TV or played all day. And after my chores were done, I would play with them.

And how we played! These were little boys with lots of energy. When toys lost their appeal, they would get up and start chasing each other around the house; bouncing and rolling marbles on the floor; or jumping up and down on the furniture.

Many times, I would be horsing around with them. One of our favourite games was playing squash in the living room — hitting a tennis ball back and forth with a racket against the walls. Of course, the ball did not always come back to us but would ricochet around. Flower vases and other items had been known to get broken during these games.

Sometimes, we would have such a rambunctious morning that one of the neighbours — usually the ones directly below us — would come up and knock on the door to tell us to settle down. This brought a few minutes of quiet, and then everything would start up again. I did not really see what the fuss was about. We had very quiet upstairs neighbours, so we never had occasion to complain. I was thinking that if we couldn't hear the folks upstairs, the ones below shouldn't hear us either. But they regularly did.

I suspected that perhaps the ones downstairs were just being mean to us. I felt persecuted. Those neighbours would come up and knock on our door for every negligible reason, including the time I allowed the boys to play in a full bathtub. We immediately heard about it.

Knock, knock, excuse me, your bathroom is leaking. Can you fix that? We fixed it, but to get even, we had a very noisy game of marbles in the living room after the bath.

Another game we loved was play-acting. The boys enjoyed taking on roles from the bible, no doubt something they learned during Sunday school, and of course, I mostly got the supporting role.

One day, we decided to enact a scene from David and Goliath. Everyone naturally wanted to be David. I wanted to be David too. To settle this matter, we staged the play three times. But when my turn came to play David, the boys' attention had started to wander and they had forgotten their lines, so I was left to do a minimalist version.

Dialogue? Bah! As I was getting ready for action, my right hand man pushed me towards Goliath, who was now standing on a sofa with a really mean look in his eye. "Go, go."

"Hey, don't I get to say anything?" I stumbled forward. Goliath took this movement to mean I had released the slingshot, so he would topple on the floor and die. Thus ended my much-awaited acting part. Oh, the unfairness of it all! But we enjoyed doing this and ultimately we all collapsed on the floor laughing.

Sundays were church days, and Bossy and I woke up earlier than usual. I would go down to the parking lot to wash the family car. I did this voluntarily because, as I told Bossy, I did not want my Mumsy going to church in a dirty car. After that, Bossy would go down to the nearby wet market and buy our grocery supply for the whole week. He mostly came home with fresh fish, meat and vegetables, which I would repack for cold storage in the refrigerator. Then, everyone would get ready for church. During my early days, I went with the family every Sunday to church. This was a new experience for someone like me who rarely went to church back in the Philippines.

People were friendly and they made me feel like a real member of the congregation. There was lots of singing and praying and I felt a vibrant energy emanate from the crowd. I remembered thinking that if God really existed, He was bound to be there with us during those Sunday morning worship hours.

At Marine Parade Church, I learned to pray by expressing my feelings honestly to God, not by doing rote prayers — repeated a hundred times — like I used to do. In that Marine Parade church, I felt that God was actually listening to me.

After the church service, people would loiter around awhile to share refreshments and catch up with friends. Children played together and everything would be joyful and friendly. As for me, I just sat around and soaked up the atmosphere.

After a few Sundays with my employers, I met Eliza, Arlin and Theresa. Eliza and Arlin were both Filipino workers. Theresa was Singaporean. With the help of church elder Auntie Jane Yang, we started our own Filipino fellowship. After church and lunch, we would go to bible study and a prayer session under the leadership of Auntie Jane and her son Tuck Yoong. When I was with my friends, we usually had dinner out at some hawker centre together before I return home.

This was how I filled my working days in Singapore.

(Clockwise from bottom) Marc Aw, his brother Kenny, and me.

My room at the Eunos flat.

Bossy, mumsy and Marc Aw.

Grandma and Marc Aw.

My favourite grandma.

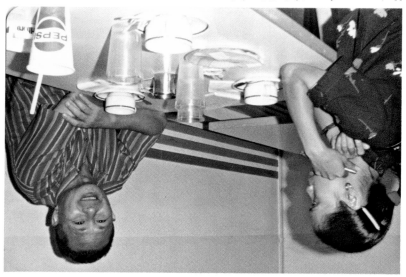

Having a cup of tea with Dr F. Landa Jocano.

Mr Fred Rosario and his family.

69

Marc Aw today.

Kenny Aw today.

(From left) Yu Shan, Fook Kwang, Bee Leng, Ming Chou and Yu Shi – with their dogs.

(From left) Maricar and Maricel.

Maricar and husband Victor Laylo, and their three children – Francis, Patricia and Charles.

Catherine and husband Robert Jones.

Crisanta Sampang today.

REACHING OUT

Every foreign worker has to live with homesickness and isolation everyday. Domestics like me are more fortunate, I think, because we could sometimes pretend our employers are our own families, although it's not quite the same. You almost always feel a need; a yearning for something more.

In Singapore, you'll see us bustling around in groups during our days off. The buses are abuzz with excited conversations in a variety of Filipino dialects, a sound so familiar to a Filipino's ear, that if one takes a moment to close her eyes, one almost feels she's back on the streets of downtown Manila. You'll find us in the malls, in the church, in the parks. I used to tell myself with some amusement that on a Sunday morning, you could throw something up into the air along Orchard Road, and it would probably land on a Filipino's head.

We go where everyone else goes. We search for familiar voices and faces in the crowds. We try to connect in various ways — we create families, we give birth to sisters, aunts, and uncles. In this foreign world, every female friend is a sister, an auntie, or an adoptive mum.

There are countless ways of reaching out to others, but it all boils down to one thing — we're all trying to find a temporary refuge from loneliness.

GOING TO CHURCH

For such a small country, Singapore has an unbelievable number of worship places that serve the faithful of every stripe. There are Catholic and Protestant churches, Muslim mosques, Buddhist, Hindu and Taoist temples, amongst others.

Everyday, in Eunos Crescent, I would pause to listen periodically as the Imam from the nearby mosque call out the time for prayers. Even though I did not understand what he was saying, his voice had a calming effect on me and every call became a marker as I moved through my working day.

Filipinos love going to church. It doesn't matter which country they're in. If there's a church, they're going to it. During my time in Singapore, there was a revival sweeping through Christian circles. We called it the Christian charismatic movement — a back-to-the-bible approach to religion. It proposed building a more personal relationship with God, and unlike the conventional practice, this new way of worship was more enjoyable and welcoming. The services were accompanied by lots of singing, drumming and guitar playing, and socialising afterwards. The churches become a lighthouse drawing lonely, homesick pilgrims looking to belong.

Filipinos are mostly Catholics, and the bulk of the domestic worker population would turn out in droves to attend masses on Sundays. There are strong contingents of these women at St. Francis Xavier in Serangoon Gardens, at the Holy Rosary Cathedral in Bras Basah, at the Catholic church in Novena and a host of others places. Others will be worshipping in the Protestant churches, or other Christian denominations. After the mass, these women would usually spend the day together, to meet with the Filipino congregation of other churches or to study the bible and have meals together. During times of need in the Philippines, like the eruption of Mount Pinatubo in 1997, these maids would be at the forefront of fundraising to help the victims back home.

My employers were devout Christians and they were members of the Marine Parade Christian Fellowship. They re-kindled my interest in the religion. I was born a Catholic, but my own family was never very religious. As a child, I remembered going with my parents to attend the Holy Mass only on Christmas Day or when a relative was getting baptised, married, or buried.

Going with the Aw family every Sunday was a new experience. We sang praises and gospel songs, we prayed, we shared personal stories of what God had done for us through the week. We talked about the teachings of the bible.

The children went to Sunday school while the adults attended the regular services. Afterwards, we came together to catch up on what else was happening in each other's lives, and partake of the refreshments. This was called "fellowshipping." The whole thing started at 10 am in the morning and would go on until around lunchtime. For lunch, before my own group became established, I went with the family to Grandma's or to the hawker centre. After I acquired my own circle of friends, my employers allowed me to spend the day with them to pursue other activities.

VOID DECK FRIENDSHIPS

Many apartment buildings in Singapore have void decks — big open spaces where concrete benches and tables have been constructed to encourage residents to mix and mingle. This is where everyone, including children and their nannies, could sit around and play games whenever they wanted to.

Like other maids, my friends and I took our charges to the void deck everyday. In the mornings and again in the afternoons, we'd be there to wait for the school bus. Every now and then, the maids would meet and share lunch or snacks in each other's apartments, or visit the hawker centre a short distance away. Sometimes, we just sat around on the benches and talked. Out of these friendships grew lasting ties, because whenever one of these women went home, her friends will be sending money or little presents to their own families through her. Meeting each other's families took the relationship to a higher level.

SHOPPING AND OUTINGS

After attending church service in the morning, the maid's other day-off activity is going on picnics with friends at one of the many parks in Singapore. Perennial favourites included the Botanical Gardens and

Sentosa Island. Hundreds more spent their time along Orchard Road or at People's Park, scouting for bargains and hoarding their low-priced buys to send back by sea cargo or through a home-bound friend to their families back in the Philippines. Still others worked throughout the month, and only left the house to send money home or go out with their employers.

Every corner of the train station at Orchard Road would have a group of women chatting or sitting around throughout the day. Every bench at Lucky Plaza, or the staircase side of Tang's Department Store, has at least two *Pinays* (short for Filipino women) sharing the space. They catch up with each other's news for the week; they talk about their families and show each other the latest photographs they've received; they ate together at the fast food joints; they do some window shopping; they visit remittance and cargo offices to send money and stuff home, etc.

SAME-SEX RELATIONSHIPS

Same-sex relationships are common in the domestic workers' community. Away from family pressure and the judgment of friends back home, it is easier to "come out" and express oneself in another country. Some of the lesbian couples I met in Singapore actually started their relationship back in the Philippines, and the reason they got out of the country was to pursue it with more freedom. Many of these couples continued on to Canada after their contracts expire. I have several friends who were in happy lesbian relationships. These women swore that such a bonding was more satisfying than being with a man. For one thing, according to my friend Narcy, sex was better because your lesbian partner, who had a unique window into both the masculine and feminine psyches, understood your needs better. Besides, you couldn't get pregnant. By hooking up with another woman, you didn't only gain a lover; you also acquired a best friend. It was love and passion, they promised, minus the heartbreak.

ILLICIT ROMANCES

For those interested in other romantic pursuits, malls were a great place to meet prospective dates, and everybody understood that alliances formed between married lovers abroad were largely transient — at least it was supposed to be — yet many marriages in the Philippines had fallen apart because of this. (Before I elaborate on this one, let me clear one thing up, least I be pelted with stones by my angry sisters in profession — *not* all foreign maids play the dating game in Singapore.)

Despite the twice-a-year pregnancy test and the S$5,000 bond, a few maids have been known to jump merrily into bed with their boyfriends — Singaporean or otherwise — got pregnant, have abortions, or run off with someone else's husband.

I learned about these secret liaisons through conversations with friends; by shamelessly eavesdropping while on buses on weekends, or by discreetly observing others whenever I had my off-days. From my vantage point on the top step of Lucky Plaza's front entrance, I'd often watched the mating rituals of the displaced unfold before me. Many partnerships, same-sex or otherwise, had been cemented or dissolved on those steps, or in its hallways, or in adjacent fast food joints. Lucky Plaza was one of the most popular watering holes for Filipino workers.

Chatty taxi drivers were also a minefield of information. Singaporean taxi drivers were very friendly and normally well informed, and I enjoyed chatting with them. For instance, I once took a taxi to meet a friend for coffee at the Shangri-La Hotel. The taxi driver was very impressed. He told me that the maids he knew went to Geylang motels, the ultimate in low-priced dating destinations, and favoured by illicit lovers for its cheap, hourly rental rate. Apparently, some suites didn't even have a washroom. Instead, every room has a sink and a portable basin for toilet functions. Motel staff would knock on the door every hour to remind the tenants of how much time had passed. If these were all true, I didn't think it was a very romantic way to spend a day with one's lover; but I suppose when you were on a budget, you had to get used to that.

I assured the driver I was not going out on a date. Notwithstanding my insistence that I wasn't looking for a boyfriend, he handed me his card after I paid my fare. He said, "Here's my card. Whenever you feel like going *jalan-jalan*, give me a call." It was an admirably bold proposition. I could only assume he had done this before with considerable success.

One taxi dude had related the whole story of his life within the length of time we traveled from Eunos Crescent to Coronation Road. He complained that his wife never washed his clothes, nor cooked his dinner or even took care of his other personal needs. All she wanted was his money. Gimme, gimme, gimme, he said. So he got himself a girlfriend, a Filipino maid. During the whole time they were going out, the girlfriend made him so happy that he bought her jewellery and provided her with spending money regularly until the day she left Singapore. Unfortunately, the maid had now finished her contract, gone home to the Philippines, and was never coming back. It was all very interesting, I commented, but why was he telling me all these? He looked at me and smiled broadly, "I thought you might be interested in replacing her." He was so disarmingly candid I had to smile back, even as I turned his offer down.

CONSTRUCTION SITE FRIENDSHIPS

During the years that I was in Singapore, there was a construction boom in the country, and various building companies employed hundreds of Filipino workers. My fellowship brother, Arlin, worked for one such company in Woodlands.

He told us workers lived right on the premises, first on makeshift dwellings, then, when a level in the building was completed, the men were allowed to occupy it. These were called the "barracks". They moved into the rooms, furnished them with beds, portable kitchen appliances and stereo systems. These they augmented with utensils they found on their foraging trips around residential areas — looking for cast-off but still useful household things like pots, coffee makers, rice cookers or discarded pieces of good furniture. Slowly, individual rooms became home. All the place needed was a woman's touch — and provided it would be. On Saturdays and Sundays, girlfriends and lovers would descend on the site and turn the place festive. Smells of cooking and sounds of music and laughter would fill the barracks.

But in the long run, things do not always end on a happy note. Families in the Philippines broke up. Some men never went back to their wives, and some wives never went back to their husbands. There were women who turned suicidal at the end of a relationship. In cases of unwanted pregnancies, abortion procedures could go awry. Arlin told me about one of his buddies who was called away from work one day by his girlfriend, a maid, before she passed out at her own workplace. The woman had recently gone through an abortion. The procedure had been performed by some fly-by-night doctor and it did not go very well, resulting in infection and blood poisoning. Arlin's friend jumped into a taxi to his girlfriend's employer's place and took her to the hospital. The employers were notified afterwards, and they were very sympathetic and understanding. The matter was never reported to the authorities, and the girl went back to work after she got better. This maid was fortunate in many ways — she survived the ordeal, and her employers did not send her home in disgrace.

Even Arlin himself had once surrendered to this neediness. When I first saw him with Eliza, I thought they were having an affair, but I was wrong. He was actually going out with another woman, a married domestic worker from the Ilocos region. Angelina, I think her name was. Angelina had once visited our fellowship through Arlin's invitation, but she never came again. I believed Arlin broke up with her because it was too much guilt to bear, especially for a married man who went to church and communed with God every Sunday. I heard through the grapevine that Angelina suspected me of stealing her boyfriend, and promised to drag me through the streets of Singapore by the hair, then display my dead body at Lucky Plaza if she ever saw me again. I didn't steal Angelina's boyfriend, of course, but I somehow felt deliciously dangerous, having supposedly one-upped another woman.

These things come to pass because a worker needs to make a connection, in whatever ways available to her, to survive in a foreign place.

When a woman reaches out, she takes whoever it is that reaches back.

MAKING FRIENDS

Everyone needs a friend. I was no exception. In the Eunos Crescent neighbourhood, there were women who became an important part of my life for almost three years — Rose, Tina, Helen, Lalay, Paulita, Luningning and Narcy. They were my void deck friends. I've often wondered where they are now and what they are doing. These were other maids, women whom I could have kept in contact with when I left Singapore, but didn't. We lost touch when I stepped off the soil and I'm still banging my head against the wall for never having bothered to keep the various friendships I had forged. What *was* I thinking?

Two of my best void deck buddies were Narcy, and her partner, Helen. Rose and Myrna were another gay couple I used to hang out with. Unlike gay women from the West, Filipino gays prefer to project a manlier image of themselves — they dress and behave like men. My friends, who swore that gay relationships were better than straight partnerships, tried long and hard to recruit me into the sisterhood. I could have been right in there with them, except I did not want to get involved with anybody — male or female — while working abroad.

They were wrong about the "no heartbreak" promise, however. Whether gay or straight, a relationship works only if both parties are equally committed. Not long after I met Rose, she broke off with Myrna to date a younger woman. Rose's new romance lasted only a few months because Lennie, who was a devout Christian, felt guilty about going out with someone of the same sex. Rose was inconsolable for a few days, until another pretty young thing with big hair wandered into her line of vision.

Narcy and Helen's love, however, proved more durable. In 1987, Narcy went off to Toronto, Canada, to work as a nanny. Helen left Singapore to join her a few months later. Not too long after that, Narcy found an employer for me in Toronto, but I already had a family waiting in Vancouver. I sent a friend in my place, and I exchanged letters with Narcy and Helen for a long while after.

Rosario Malabanan was another friend I made in Singapore. She was one of few I'm still in close contact with, and with whom I had shared many adventures. We both went to Vancouver eventually, and we still regard each other as family. Rosario is a very special woman. She is smart, good looking, with long, brown hair and almond eyes, and she loved dressing up. One of her employers actually called her a glamour puss. But more than that, she had the strength to live up to her convictions. I remembered a very personal story she told me when we were still working in Singapore.

Rosario was employed by a couple with two young children. Her boss was a very kind, successful businessman, and Rosario had a very good relationship with him and his wife. Rosario loved her employers' children. After working for them for a while, she started to notice her boss' growing interest in her. Very often, his eyes would simply light up whenever she entered the room. He would also comment on how pretty she looked, or how nice her dress was. One day, he offered to send her back to the Philippines, and to provide her with all the necessary finances to start a business there. The offer, which was made in front of the whole family, had seemed perfectly genuine.

But Rosario knew that there could be strings attached, so she turned it down. She told them instead that she had already applied for a job in Canada. The boss, however, continued to pay court, so much so that Rosario started to feel extremely uncomfortable. The problem was finally resolved one afternoon when they were alone in one of the children's bedrooms. Her boss approached her and asked, "Can I kiss you?"

Rosario moved away, and said firmly, "No, Sir. I'm sorry."

The boss apologised and left the room. Afterwards, both of them pretended the incident never happened and her boss never asked again. Rosario was thankful that she never lost her respect for her employer. After she left the family, she kept in contact with them and they remain friends to this day. Rosario believed that a woman should never sleep with her boss, and she practised what she preached.

Outside of Eunos Crescent, at the Marine Parade Christian Centre, I have a different set of friends. Amongst these was Theresa Devasahayam. I met Theresa when she was a young sociology major at the University of Singapore. Theresa introduced me to her two Filipino friends, Arlin and Eliza, and to her elder sister, Patricia. Pat was also a university student, and a classically trained pianist. Eliza was a good-looking 40-something — a pastor in a Protestant church before she left the Philippines.

What I remembered most about Eliza was her encyclopaedic knowledge of the bible. During our bible study sessions, everyone had a book from which we read the different verses. Eliza seemed to remember all these verses by heart, word for word; their numbers, titles and chapters. She was a fountain of verses, a veritable walking and talking bible — the modern King James Version — spouting teachings and parables without once checking them up in her own book. I was in awe each time I listened to her. I secretly aspired to be like her, but lacked the requisite dedication to attain it.

Arlin was also in his 40s, a quiet, big-brotherly kind of guy. I had a big crush on Arlin, but he and Eliza were very close. They always left the bible study sessions together. Before I came to know them, I suspected that they were having an affair.

Together, we formed the core of the Marine Parade Filipino Fellowship. Our worship leaders were all elders of our church. There was Auntie Jane Yang, David Alphonso, and Uncle Chua Peng Cheng. Patricia Devasahayam would accompany us on the piano while we sang praises. We were all on fire for the Lord. It was a label that born-again people put on each other's enthusiasm about sharing the word of God with the rest of the world. Like them, I looked forward to going to church every Sunday.

We invited every Filipino we met on our forays around town. Many of them came and a lot of them stayed with us for as long as they could — maids, construction workers, sailors, and the odd tourist. Theresa even brought a visiting Filipino professor — a well-known author and sociologist, Dr F. Landa Jocano, from the University of the Philippines. He was an unassuming man, like someone's favourite uncle.

Dr Jocano encouraged me to go back to the Philippines to finish my studies. He promised to help me obtain a research assistant's job at the University, so that I could do a Master's in Sociology. I loved the thought. But by then, I had Canada on my mind. I would never forget his argument. He had said, "You will get to Vancouver one day, if that's where you want to go. I've always believed that if you do what you love, money will follow. Look at me."

Dr Jocano pointed out what an important opportunity it was he had offered me. Working with him on the intellectual level was a once-in-a-lifetime chance that many students would kill for. (It never ceased to amaze me how often residing in another country becomes a great equaliser among Filipinos. Had I been a regular student in the Philippines, Dr Jocano and I wouldn't be drinking coca cola together and hanging out at Lucky Plaza like old buddies. I would have had to go through a phalanx of assistants in his University of the Philippines offices to get near him.)

I felt both very grateful and humbled for being chosen, even as I turned down his invitation. It was a tempting offer, and I gave it a lot of serious thought, but my prime focus was the future of my children. I didn't want to take a chance, and gamble away the future. Security was my major concern. Academic excellence may or may not better my life, but I knew a job in Canada certainly would. I was the head of a little family whose fortunes were totally tied to mine.

I chose the surer path.

Every once in a while, I would wonder about this — the road not taken. I would brood about it, with some regret, although honestly, I have never been able to picture myself as an academic, debating the merits of triage or the tragedy of the commons with my students.

But I digress. Of my friends, Theresa was by far the most hardworking. On some weekday nights, Theresa would sleep over at our place and do her homework. She would work late into the night. Her drive and determination surpassed that of most students. For Theresa, it was an "A" grade or nothing.

On some evenings, I brought all three of them, Arlin, Eliza and Theresa, home for dinner. They were always welcomed, and were treated by my employers like members of the family. I remain grateful to Bossy and Mumsy for those times, because I rarely heard about other families doing the same thing for their maids.

I did have a secret crush on Arlin, but having an affair with anyone, including him, was the last thing on my mind, for two reasons: At 27, I have dumped one husband, raised three children, and consequently, have become totally disillusioned with marriage and relationships. I swore I would dedicate my whole life to raising my kids and not give anything more than cursory attention to those philandering, boozing, irresponsible, worthless members of the opposite sex. Of course, I've had to revise my opinion regarding men several times over... but that came later.

Out of my affection for Arlin came a poem I wrote for *The Straits Times*, called, "From a House-maiden to Her Construction Man". It was the first ever, and so far the last, set of rhymes I ever wrote in my life. I didn't know if Arlin knew it was his poem, but according to him, it proved a hit with all the construction workers on his worksite, so much so that they made it their anthem. Arlin told me that almost every room in his hostel had a clipping of the poem posted on the wall.

Two years later, the Marine Parade Filipino Fellowship disbanded. Things changed after Patricia went off to do her post-graduate studies at the University of Hawaii in the United States. Arlin went back to the Philippines. Eliza left to join another worship group downtown. Not too long after, Theresa visited Patricia in Hawaii. I met new maids and made new friends, but no one was able to take Theresa's, or Arlin's or Eliza's place in my life. I still miss them. The lessons I learned during the times we were together were lasting, and I was grateful to the Marine Parade Christian Centre for helping me find spiritual renewal in Singapore.

MAID AND BUDDING WRITER

One wise man — I forgot who it was — once wrote that if you read, it followed that one day you would want to write. My sentiment, exactly.

I grew up in a household that loved to read. My parents were avid readers. Our house was littered with Tagalog weeklies and old books. My mother regularly bought and exchanged *Bulaklak* and *Liwayway* magazines with other readers in the village. Those were the days before television, and a person had to invent his own means of entertainment. One of my favorite comic stories from *Bulaklak* was Dyesebel, a mermaid who battled the evil forces in the sea. I learned to read at four, just because everyone around was too busy doing their own reading to pay attention to me.

One day, while keeping my mother company as she washed our clothes in the creek, I decided to ask her for help. Syllable by syllable, my mother read me one of the stories. By the time she was done with the washing, I was reading all by myself. The first story I learned to read was called *Dagitab* — a science-fiction piece about a man who gained superpower after being zapped in an electric chair. I've never stopped reading ever since.

My father, too, loved reading and telling stories. The lullabies he sang to me when I was little were about magical places and their kings and queens and princes and princesses. He called them "Corido". He would often sing to me on demand, even after I was too old for lullabies. Father had also related a few tall stories in his time — encounters with the *tikbalangs* — the Filipino equivalent of trolls; and the *engkantos* — powerful mythical beings who can take human form — living in the forest at the edge of our farm while night fishing with his brothers. He could have been a great writer.

As a student in the city, I used to skip classes whenever the time came to pay school fees. I would inevitably have run out of money, so

I would spend such days camped out at a relative's house. Everybody would be at work, and my aunt Marietta was then away attending college in Manila so I was free to help myself to all of her books.

In her room, I happily explored the world of the ancient Greeks and their gods, in the *Iliad* and the *Odyssey*. I got lost in Perry Mason's maze of legal cases. I read an endless stream of *Readers' Digest* magazines and collections of poetry written by various English and American poets. My school attendance went down but my command of English gained a big boost. On days when I actually showed up in school, I excelled in writing and aced my English exams.

When I was older, I would go home once in a while to visit my parents and perhaps coax some extra spending money out of them. After my father became bedridden, it was my turn to tell him stories. He loved martial tales, and during the times that I visited them in the village, I'd bring my own copy of the *Iliad* and read it to him, translating it into Tagalog as I went along. Father listened attentively to accounts of the Trojan War, the shenanigans of the ancient Greek gods and the adventures of their human pawns.

So I grew up with an incurable reading habit. My head was filled with words and stories, some of which were my own creation. I fantasised that one day I would capture these thoughts buzzing around like mosquitoes inside my head and put them down on paper. I dreamt and schemed for years, but I never expected that I would first have to work as a domestic in Singapore before finding my voice.

After arriving in Singapore, I started reading *The Straits Times* everyday. I would read every page, but I paid special attention to the human interest, arts and leisure sections. I wanted to be informed about what was happening around me; more so, I wanted to understand Singapore's culture and its people because it was my new home. I even joined a lipogram contest through a column called "At Large", written by Mr David Kraal, then associate editor of *The Straits Times*. The contest required every entrant to describe him/herself without using the letter "e". I was thrilled no end when he mentioned my name in his column. At the time, I had thought that referring to my own eyes as "ocular organs" was a stroke of genius. Now, however, I realised that must have been incredibly corny.

I found something to write about after my first year in Singapore. I was so impressed with working life here, and how it slowly changed my attitude, that I borrowed Bossy's typewriter and wrote a story titled, "Singapore, Mahal Kita". This I promptly sent to *The Straits Times'* lifestyle section. The editor liked it, and he sent a photographer down to take pictures of my Singaporean family. A few days later, there it was, my very own writing in print. Marc, Kenny and I were in the picture, playing together, with Bossy and Mumsy reading the papers in the background. I was unbelievably proud of myself. It was the first story I've ever written in my life. It wasn't a scintillating, literary piece. In fact, it was even somewhat cliché ridden, but it expressed my deepest feelings, and the newspaper thought it was good enough to share with its readers. Well, that was good enough for me.

My next contribution to the paper was inspired by an article written by Mr Richard Lim. I did not know then that he worked for *The Straits Times*, but he had written a very entertaining account of his experiences as a would-be Buddhist acolyte in a temple in Japan, in the column "Personal Glimpses". Before this, I didn't even know I had a sense of humour, but as I re-read Lim's article, I started thinking that perhaps I, too, could write something like this. I went back to my borrowed typewriter and hammered out a description of my experiences with my Eunos Crescent family. I sent it to the same newspaper section and it was published two weeks later. Thanks to Richard Lim, writing out this second story was much easier. I credit Richard with having seriously inspired my next wave of writings.

I remembered very clearly the first time I spoke to Richard on the phone. I was mopping the floor when the call came. I propped my mop against the wall and grabbed the phone.

Imagine my disbelief as I listened to something that sounded like this:

"This is Richard Lim from *The Straits Times*. Can I talk to Crisanta Sampang, please?"

Richard Lim? The man himself? OH. MY. GOD. As my heart was doing a double somersault, I calmly spoke into the phone, " This is Crisanta. One minute, please."

I covered the receiver tightly with my other hand and held it away from me, then let out a loud, sustained scream that lasted many seconds. I could tell Richard heard the whole thing because I detected laughter in his voice when we resumed our conversation. He called to see if I was keen on an assignment — to review a play called *Esperanza*, the story of a Filipino domestic worker in Singapore who had the misfortune of finding an abusive employer. Richard wanted my emotional reaction to the play, not a technical review of it. A group of Singaporeans produced and acted in it. He was sending me two tickets to the play and he would be sitting on the same row of seats. I was going to meet RL in person! Towards the end of our conversation, enough adrenaline had pumped into my brain and turned it into mush.

Richard sent me the tickets that same afternoon. Being in receipt of those tickets made me feel genuinely professional. I was overjoyed. What can I say? I just talked to Mr Inspiration himself, who gave me a writing assignment. I was just this maid, a village kid, a farmer's daughter from a hick town in the Philippines, and I was being given a chance to write for someone who had been in the business for years. I floated in the stratosphere for a whole week.

I frantically called my cousin Santa to invite her to the play but she wasn't available. Nobody else was, except Arlin, and I spent the whole evening seated between him and Richard Lim. I regretted taking Arlin to the play, but what was a girl to do. Richard and I talked a little bit before I turned my attention to the stage. After all, I was there to watch *Esperanza* and to allow my feelings about her rise to the surface.

I liked the play. *Esperanza* was well-written, well-performed, and extensively researched. It captured the nuances of a Filipino domestic's life in Singapore. It mirrored the isolation, the sacrifices and the cultural shock that a maid could suffer in an unfortunate working environment, as well as every migrant worker's hopes about the future that refused to die. I thought it was like a bridge that, when crossed with an open mind, could make both employers and maids understand each other better. It had one basic flaw, however: the play was bleak from beginning to end. To my mind, it lacked balance. It failed to mention all the other good employers that were alive and well in Singapore.

After *Esperanza*, my writing started attracting some outside attention. This included the National Teachers Union of Singapore who approached me to contribute to their publication. Mr Swithun Lowe, the National Teacher's Union representative, told me that getting stories like mine published in their magazine was a good way for teachers to understand other cultures. For them, I wrote a piece about my return to the Philippines after two years in Singapore and how the village had welcomed me.

After that, however, I had not been able to produce anything more because the ideas dried up. I was too new at writing, and during those days, I could only write when the spirit moved me. I found out much later that becoming a productive writer required a great amount of discipline. It meant having to sit in front of your typewriter everyday, having to write something even if it read like a busload of crap; sitting there and writing even if wringing words out of your brain seemed like squeezing blood from rocks. Whatever it takes, you should sit there and write, and then write some more, until the words flow and the imagination catches fire.

I received another invitation to write from *DepthNews Asia*, a news agency that distributed its articles all over the world. Mr Fred Rosario of the Philippine Embassy in Singapore sent them copies of what I had written and they liked it. Again, I never sent them anything because

I did not feel capable of doing news features. I also knew that news writing entailed a lot of research and legwork, something that would take me away from my real job. I wasn't prepared to do that.

Towards the end of 1986, Brother Mike Panganiban, a Catholic clergy from a seminary in Abra, Philippines, visited Singapore. Brother Mike's office published a worldwide newsletter for Filipino migrant workers. He came to Singapore to introduce the paper, gather subscriptions and look for contributors. He looked me up and asked me to write for his publication. It was called *Tinig Ng Bayan — People's Voices* — and was mailed monthly to international subscribers. I agreed to write for Brother Mike because I wanted to read and hear from others like me. Working for *Tinig Ng Bayan* was totally voluntary, but it was a very fulfilling experience. The quality of writing was varied, but the paper never pretended to be anything more than what it said it was — a forum for Filipinos who had left the country for distant shores. Through *Voices*, I received letters from Filipino workers all over the world — from Taiwan, Hong Kong, Italy and the Middle East. Women wrote to me saying, "thank you for putting our feelings into words ..." Men had something else to say. One Filipino civil engineer from Saudi Arabia even proposed marriage.

One day in Lucky Plaza, I experienced my first "Nora Aunor moment" — Nora Aunor was the Philippines' number one movie star when I was a teenager. It happened on a Sunday afternoon. A group of Filipino women were standing around close to us and I noticed they had been watching me for sometime. Several minutes later, one of them finally approached us. She introduced herself as Clara, and asked for my name. After making sure that I was really who she thought I was, Clara told me that she and her companions were Filipino domestics working in Brunei. They were in Singapore on holiday. *The Straits Times* was available daily in the country and she had read every article I wrote for the paper. Clara and her friends had been hoping to meet me on this trip. So we chatted, shared experiences, and posed for pictures together. I was as excited as they were with this providential meeting. Hey, I had readers in Brunei! That discovery had meant a great deal to me.

At the end of 1986, I was one of the contributors mentioned at *The Straits Times* year-ender. An editor told me that I had been receiving a lot of reader mail addressed to the paper. What I found most inspiring in all of these was that people recognised me on the streets, and told me how they had felt about my writings. The recognition felt really good, but hearing that I have touched these readers with my words counted so much more. It was a happy yet humbling feeling, because for the first time, I was ready to accept that maybe, I could actually become the writer I've always wanted to be.

Thus started my writing career. I owe *The Straits Times* a debt of gratitude, for helping me find the "write stuff" in myself, and to my Singapore family, for their support and understanding. I couldn't have done it without their permission. Mumsy and Bossy most of all — I knew they were both proud of what I did. In return, I tried my best to ensure that my affair with the typewriter never interfered with my day job.

SHELTERING
FROM THE STORM

The world is not always a kindly place, especially for domestic workers. There's bound to be a little unhappiness bubbling up somewhere. Even in the so-called developed West, abuses are not unheard of. *Walrus Magazine* in March 2005 quoted a 2000 study conducted by INTERCEDE, citing abuses that ranged from rape and sexual harassment to threats of deportation. INTERCEDE, a women's advocacy group based in Toronto, had been studying the Live-in Caregiver Programme.

In Singapore, notwithstanding its endless sunny days, despite its thousands of good employers and all those contented maids working for them, there are still a number of dissenting voices.

So where does a disgruntled maid go when she quits her job, whether out of homesickness, culture shock or employer problems? One could always go back home and be done with it. When I was working as a domestic in Singapore in the 80s, troubled maids who wanted a second chance had three options. They could either approach the Singapore authorities; ask for help at the Philippine Community Centre, or seek aid from the Geylang Catholic Centre for Migrant Workers.

THE PHILIPPINE COMMUNITY CENTRE

The Philippine Community Centre, established by President Cory Aquino in 1987, was located at 95 University Road in Singapore. The President did this with permission from the Singapore government and with money provided by the Philippine Welfare Fund Administration. The Labour Attaché oversaw its operations.

When President Cory Aquino visited Singapore in August of 1987, she announced her plan for building such a Centre to a cheering Filipino audience at Kallang Theatre. I cheered along with them although I had my doubts. I had grown cynical about political promises. Can you blame me? I grew up during the martial law years, under a government administration whose little achievements were magnified by its propaganda machinery, and all these went on even as the country drowned in debt.

That was of course before Cory Aquino's time, but I still found it hard to believe she could pull it off. I knew she meant well, but she had more pressing problems to deal with inside the Philippines, more than trying to set up a community centre in a foreign country. Well, I was wrong. The lady kept her word. Three months later, on November 30, the centre was inaugurated. By December 3, its doors were opened to Filipinos in Singapore.

On Christmas Day in 1987, armed with the Labour Attaché's invitation, I decided to check the place out. Unfortunately, I got lost along the way, having alighted at the wrong bus stop. Within minutes, I was perspiring and my feet were sore from walking up one street and down another. Swearing under my breath, I continued my search for 95 University Road for a good 45 minutes, until I saw a Singaporean woman walking with her two children and her Filipino maid. I asked her for directions and she pointed me towards a simple semi-detached house a block away.

My first visit to No 95 was a special one for two reasons. Firstly, it was my very first look at a place I never thought I would see take shape. Secondly, it was Christmas Day. The place was crawling with Filipino women. I stopped by the door and started taking my clogs off. A voice called out, "Leave them on!"

"Can?"

I wanted to be sure. Two and a half years working for a Singaporean family has taught me new habits. I walked in, clogs and all. The place seemed bright and happy. I could barely hear above the din of a hundred voices, mixed with familiar strains of a pop song coming from the stereo set, and the sounds of a Filipino film playing on video somewhere. Newspapers and magazines from home were displayed on the coffee table. Leading off from the sitting room was the dining area. There, I saw a huge dining table that was draped with a very colourful tablecloth. Chairs were lined all along the walls. Smiles everywhere. More laughter and chatting were going on in the kitchen, where a group of bustling women were preparing a party spread.

Let me tell you, the Filipinos certainly know how to eat on festive days! There were piles of sandwiches, bowls of chicken-and-macaroni salad. There were pots of rice, *adobo* and a platter of *lechon*, and even some *pancit*. Pitchers of cool orange juice were already being served. Dessert would be caramel custard.

Mr Fred Rosario arrived with his family and walked into the kitchen beaming like a proud father. The centre, he told me later, was the realisation of a dream he'd always held, ever since he was posted to Singapore in 1985. When he first came, he saw Filipino men and women hanging around shopping centres on Sundays. They all seemed to be having a good time, but, he thought, wouldn't they be better off having a common meeting place they could call their own? The then Ambassador to Singapore, Mr Frank Benedicto, helped him obtain President Aquino's support, and the Philippine Community Centre was born.

The second level of the Centre was divided into four bedrooms. Several maids were staying there that December. Two of these had been brought in by their employers. The others had run away from their host families, for reasons ranging from alleged rape, non-payment of salary to ill-treatment.

Mr Jose Sarmiento, who headed the Welfare Fund Administration, told me, "The girls will stay here while waiting for these tangles to be resolved. They may have to go home from here, move on to new employers, or return to their former ones."

Mr Fred Rosario, on the other hand, personally sifted through the many complaints and counter-complaints from Filipino workers and

their Singaporean employers. He tried to find the real reasons behind their discord, conducting endless sessions with harassed maids and angry bosses. As soon as a maid showed up at the centre, Mr Rosario would notify the employer and schedule a meeting. He arranged for them to talk in his office, and acted as a mediator when arguments broke out. There were times when the maid had to return to her former employer, and Mr Rosario was thankful for the latter's understanding when this happened.

Mr Rosario assured me that the centre did not condone or encourage maids to run away from their problems. But whether the centre was there or not, he knew that some domestic workers would leave when unhappy, and he heard that there had been times when, having no place to go, they would end up sleeping on the streets. He did not want that to happen. Everyone was welcomed at the centre. However, he warned the women that he was very strict in dealing with runaway cases. The maids should not abuse the hospitality of the place and anyone found to be untruthful would be reprimanded and repatriated to the Philippines immediately.

On my subsequent visits to the Centre, I talked to some of the runaways. One woman, aged 35, told me that she had left her workplace after seven months of service because she was only paid a fraction of the agreed salary. Why wait seven months before doing something about it, I asked.

"The family was good to me," she replied, "and they regularly gave me some pocket money. They offered credible excuses for not paying me right away. It took me seven months to realise that I was being conned."

Another maid was suspected of stealing $12,000 from her employers. The theft was never proven but her employers brought her to the centre anyway. One girl — let's call her Imelda — had shown me bruises all over her body. She alleged that her employer's brother hit her repeatedly whenever he got drunk. One day, he handed her his knife and told her to kill herself. She fled to the centre. When I talked to her, Imelda was visibly upset and very frightened. I remembered Imelda's case very well because she came from the same province as I did, and her story of ragged poverty sounded so much like mine. I went home that night thinking of different ways I might help her. After all, I could have been Imelda. But I was a step too late. The next day, I was told Imelda killed herself by jumping out of the hospital window.

Imelda wasn't the only maid who suffered at the hands of unscrupulous employers. There was a spunky woman at the Centre, who told me she had not been paid her for four months. When she approached her employer, the latter wrote out a cheque for S$1,000. Wanting cash instead, this maid tore up the cheque, and took her case to the local police. When the case reached Mr Rosario's office, he discovered that the maid's work permit had been issued under her employer's brother's name. That brought a new twist to the tale — illegal employment.

Then, there was the alleged rape victim. The girl, who was about 21, claimed that she had been sexually assaulted three times in one year by her employer's son. Her case was still pending when I left Singapore.

By the middle of January, 1988, 63 women had passed through the doors of the Philippine Community Centre. Of these, 13 were repatriated, 11 were hired by new employers, 15 cases were pending while the rest went back to their original employers. Mr Rosario told me then that he would like to add more rooms to the Centre, perhaps one for sports and games, and maybe even a corner for Filipino food stalls — a little Philippines if you will. It did not happen, but what he had achieved at the Centre was significant, and it was good enough for the women who found refuge there.

THE GEYLANG CATHOLIC CENTRE

The Geylang Catholic Centre (GCC) for Immigrant Workers, later renamed Catholic Centre for Foreign Workers, was just as welcoming, although it had a shorter shelf life. I never had a chance to visit the place, but I had read about it in the newspapers.

The GCC was a crises centre established in April 1984 by the Catholic Church in Singapore, in response to the plight of some foreign domestic workers, who had suffered abuse of one kind or another. Located in the Geylang area, the centre was run by Father Gillaume Arotcarena, 42, a Basque priest who had been living in Singapore since 1972. The centre provided refuge to maids who run away from their employers, and it offered counselling, information and legal aid services. Volunteers ran English and music classes, and often organised social functions and outdoor activities for foreign workers.

The Catholic Centre investigated at least five instances of reported employer abuse a week and housed between 10 and 15 runaway maids at any given time. By March of 1986, according to a *Sunday Times* article, Father Arotcarena had listened to over 500 complaints from aggrieved maids.

Based on the cases handled by the Centre, Father Arotcarena and two others, Dr Thomas Tan and Wong Hoe Fang, co-authored *The Maid Tangle*, a book that detailed the abuses experienced by domestic workers who came to the Geylang Catholic Centre for help. The book, launched on March 30, 1986, called for more legal protection for foreign maids.

In an interview with *The Straits Times*, a Labour Ministry spokesperson admitted that the Employment Act did not have adequate protection for domestic servants, because it was not easy to define a live-in help's working hours. Throughout the day, he said, a maid performed her work and at the same time, also did her own personal things. For example, a maid who cooked for the family was also cooking for herself. But where the law clearly defined these workers' rights, the Ministry did take actions to protect them. The office had helped resolve at least 250 cases that were referred to them by the Geylang Catholic Centre.

Unfortunately, the GCC did not remain open for long. In May, 1987, the Home Affairs Ministry announced that it had uncovered a Marxist conspiracy to overthrow the Government. The conspiracy was orchestrated, according to the Ministry, by Tan Wah Piow, 35, a Singaporean and Marxist who left Singapore in 1976 to avoid serving national service. His main man in the country was Vincent Cheng, a full time lay worker at the Geylang Catholic Centre.

The Ministry added that in 1983, Tan Wah Piow and Vincent Cheng established the English-language drama group, Third Stage, as a front.

The Third Stage had produced the play, *Esperanza*, in 1986. The two men had also apparently infiltrated several Christian groups and student organisations in the country, one of which was the Geylang Catholic Centre for Foreign Workers.

A few days later, I woke up to news reports that the Catholic Centre had closed down. Seven Filipino maids were transferred to the Philippine Embassy. Father Gillaume Arotcarena resigned from his position as director of the Centre. Vincent Cheng and several other workers and volunteers from the Centre were arrested, together with members of the Third Stage.

I kept reading until my eyes burned with uncried tears. It was a sad ending to a place which held so much promise, and which had helped so many needy women. But like the constituency it sought to serve, the Centre became a tool for people with hidden agendas; it was used and abused, laying waste to all its good intentions.

BACK TO BATANGAS

Two years were over. My contract was up and I was going home. I could hardly wait to hold my babies once again. According to the terms of my contract, my employer would provide the airfare money and they had the option of re-hiring me, or look for another maid. Mumsy and Bossy paid my airfare and asked me to return for a second term.

A lot had happened since I first landed in Singapore. I have changed so much that even I could barely recognise myself. I have evolved from being a desperate person into a happy, confident and secured individual. This time, I knew where I was going, and what I will do when I get there. I felt useful, knowing that I was providing for my family. My children and I could look forward to a more secured future.

Getting ready to go home took weeks of preparation — and two years of anticipation. The truth was, I was ready to go home everyday, if that were possible. Bit by bit, I hoarded chocolate bars, candies, hand-me-downs from Mumsy, toothpaste, bath soaps and bottles of shampoo. I also bought imported cigarettes (Blue Seal, they called it) for my brothers, and toothbrushes and dental floss for the girls (One of the things I feel passionate about is healthy teeth!) I also accumulated three umbrellas. I remembered, when I was a kid going to school ... each time it rained, I had to stand under the nearest tree or shelter, waiting for the rain to let up, because I had no umbrella. In fact, I don't remember having any umbrella during my entire student years. My girls will have as many umbrellas as they need.

A day before I left, I bought apples and oranges and grapes and stored them in a specially packed, carry-on luggage, so that they wouldn't be smashed in the cargo hold of the plane. Long before the date arrived, I wrote to my family and instructed them on how to deal with my arrival. I did not want any crowd waiting for me at the airport. Instead, I asked for one of my big brothers to meet me and help me carry my stuff home. Mumsy and the rest of the family saw me off to the airport.

Getting on a plane was still exciting as this was only my second time. While waiting to board my flight, I entertained myself by walking around the airport and looking at the stores. Changi Airport was, and remained to me, a great place, because of its variety of shops, its fresh orchids and greenery decorating the place.

Finally, I was on the Manila-bound flight. Many of the travelers were Filipinos, with a few others of various nationalities. A lot of the women were domestic helpers going back for a visit or leaving Singapore for good. There were Filipino sailors as well. We passed the time by talking to one another, exchanging telephone numbers or addresses. Before long, our plane was touching down at the Manila International Airport. When the plane finally stopped, a Filipino song was played, and the passengers, every one of them as excited as I was, applauded and cheered. A few seconds after that, everything else was forgotten, as each and everyone rushed out of the plane into the arms of our waiting families.

Kuya Edo, my second big brother, came with one of our cousins to pick me up from the airport. We boarded a passenger jeepney to the provincial bus station, transferred to one bound for Lipa, and waited for it to leave. I stared impatiently out the bus window, imagining how much my daughters have grown and how they would look like today. I felt a gaping emptiness that widened with every passing second. Taking public transport was starting to seem like a really bad idea. Every inch of my body ached to hold my daughters close. My mother was not very good with sending photographs, or writing letters, and despite my repeated nagging, all I received was one solitary picture of the three: Maricel, Maricar, and Catherine, posing with two of their similar-aged cousins.

All three were dressed in pretty, matching outfits, but what broke my heart was the sadness in their eyes. Catherine, especially, whose big brown eyes could never hide whatever she was feeling. I cried the first time I looked at the photograph.

Sitting there, however, gave me a chance to look around the bus station. God, it seemed so different from when I left. Everyone, everything, seemed disorganised. There were so many people milling around. Everybody was either a passenger or a vendor trying to sell something. The bus station was a swirling, swarming, fluid, marketplace. Was it me, I thought crossly, or had it always been like this? Finally, the bus driver got behind the wheels and we were on our way. I heaved a sigh of relief, then sat back to watch the scenery outside my window.

Two hours later, we arrived at my hometown. When we reached the depot, several village jeepneys were still waiting for passengers. I refused to wait another minute, so we paid for the estimated number of people that would fill the jeepney on its regular run and off we went — through the town, onto the highway, then finally, we were bouncing along graveled road that led into the villages. Outside, the seemingly endless sugarcane fields zipped by, as unchanging and faded as when I left. As we entered my village, a few people along the road recognised me and waved, and I waved back.

I was home.

When the jeepney stopped, there stood waiting for me on the roadside, my mother, my big sister *Ate* Janing, and my *Kuya* Fernando. I jumped out to hug my mother, forgetting to pay the driver, leaving *Kuya* Edo to deal with him. As we walked down the path though the trees into the house, who should come running towards me at warp speed but my three little ones!

Maricel led the pack, screaming happily. I dropped my luggage and opened my arms wide. Maricel went airborne, threw her arms around my neck, her legs around my waist, with a force that nearly toppled us both. Then came Maricar, a little more subdued but no less welcoming, hugging me wordlessly. Then Catherine came along — plump, brown-skinned, four and a half years old, with long hair and laughing brown eyes.

I tried frantically to fit all three of them in my embrace, thinking, my god, my god, how much they have grown! There were kisses and hugs all around. All of a sudden, I seemed to have grown three permanent appendages, one tightly attached to my arm; another at my waistline and yet a third clinging to my clothes. Someone — I didn't remember who — picked up my luggages and we all hobbled home together.

I had come home to a new residence. Over the past two years, my mother, god bless her, had been wisely saving some of the money I sent her every month, and had bought us a piece of land in the village proper. We used to live on a corner of our old farm, which had long since been sold, but the new owners had allowed us to remain on the place, as we had nowhere else to go. Mother had our old house torn down and rebuilt in this new lot. A new kitchen and living room were also added. Mother, *Kuya* Fernando, the girls and *Kuya* Toto, the itinerant son who worked off and on as an electrician in Manila, all lived in the same house now.

The land area was large enough to accommodate a second, smaller house, which was built by my sister Janing and her family. Through my mother's prudence, I would also acquire the adjacent lot, which my brother would later clear. On this plot will be planted black pepper vines and vegetables. The house was surrounded by coffee, star apple (or "caimito", an indigenous product of the Philippines) and coconut trees. The place was nothing like the farm I grew up in, but we own it now, and that made it special. I felt suddenly like a real grown-up.

Finally, I was providing for my mother. I was able to give her some financial freedom. Right now, she didn't have to worry anymore about where the next meal was coming from.

The old house was reassembled differently, but the basic materials were there: the sheets of corrugated iron roofing, the woven bamboo walls and split bamboo flooring. My father's antique four-poster bed sat in one corner of the communal bedroom. It was a squeeze for everyone to be living in the same house, especially the sleeping quarters, but it felt good to have one's very own place. I remain grateful to my mother for having spent my Singapore earnings wisely. Although I did not realise it at that time, but as my children grew up, having our own place became more important.

In retrospect, I committed the same "sins", or sacrifices, my parents did when I was younger. I failed to understand the significance of what I did until much later. In my desire to prepare for my children a life that was different from mine, I did the exact same thing that my parents did to me: I left my kids to the care of others. I left them motherless. I left them with my mother, all the while comforting myself that at least, they wouldn't have to live with some distant relative, like I did when I was younger.

My girls told me nothing; they never complained. I thought everything was all right. I should have taken a cue from a letter Catherine wrote to me when she was eight years old. She had said, "*Wag mo na lang akong ibili ng Barbie, uwi ka na lang.*" (I don't need you to buy me a Barbie, I just want you to come home.) Two decades later, I learned from them that growing up without Mother was not much fun at all, even when a doting grandmother was around to attend to their every need. But I digress...

I climbed up into the communal bedroom area, which doubled up as living quarters in the daytime. It looked down into the sitting room, where the floor was laid with packed earth. There were various items of humble furniture: our old dining table with two benches on both sides, as well as bamboo benches along one entire wall for visitors to sit on. My mother didn't manage to save enough for new furniture. The kitchen was in the next room, separated by a wall of woven bamboo strips (We call it *sawali*). In the kitchen were a big wood stove and several cupboards to store plates and such. There was also a counter for preparing food.

Looking around, I remembered my father's last days and I felt a pain that went right through my chest. I wish Father had been here to meet me. I wish he was able to see that I was trying to live out his dream for me and that I was now taking care of my mother. Father loved my mother exceedingly and he had worried about how she would fare when he was gone. His last instruction to his children before he died was, "I want you all to look after your mother and treat her well. If I ever see her cry because of any of you, I will come back and make your lives miserable." It was a half-joke, but I knew he meant it.

I turned my attention to my other family members and examined them surreptitiously. *Kuya* Fernando now walked with a limp, as a result of the accident that broke his leg two years ago, but he was pleased to see me. My mother seemed not to have aged very much, and she seemed more relaxed than I remembered. My big sister hadn't aged a day either. *Kuya* Toto, who had always been different, was standing quietly to one side. He acknowledged my arrival with a smile and a nod. My eldest brother, who lived in another town, hadn't arrived.

My brother-in-law, Nicasio, my sister's husband, was also there with their little girl, Bess. They had erected their little house next door to ours. Nicasio is the ultimate do-it-yourself man. He built their house from scratch, and you could tell it was tiny, but the craftsmanship was impressive. It reminded me of a hobbit's house — small, just right for people who were no taller than five feet and a half. The bamboo floors were polished, and every other detail was just right.

Nicasio is technically gifted. He learned to repair stereo systems just by taking one apart and then putting it back together. He was also a self-taught electrician. He acquired the skill by working with *Kuya* Toto and watching what he did. Nicasio became such a good electrician that he now does all the electrical installation works in the village. He was just a sugarcane field worker when I left two years ago.

I noticed the house was slowly filling up with people — other relatives, friends, neighbours and their children.

I asked my mother to brew some coffee, and what did she say?

"Oh, we don't have coffee. Didn't think about buying any."

Aside from having no coffee, there was no other food in the house except rice, so I gave her some money and someone ran up to the store to get canned sardines, coffee, sugar and other things for dinner. I was secretly annoyed at that, but then I realised that these guys were just being true to form — laid back, somewhat disorganised, aside from being very excited because I was coming home. Trust my mother not to think about getting supper ready for her homecoming little girl. I even suspected she was hoping I would stop by the public market to pick up groceries. The thought annoyed me a little bit more, because she was so wrong. Going to market never crossed my mind, at any instance between the airport and home. Now we had to eat rice and sautéed canned sardines for dinner, which wasn't too bad, except that no one was thinking about food or cooking except me amidst the chaos in the house.

Kuya Fernando nudged me to ask for some money. His friends had started arriving and he was proud to entertain them, because his little sister was back from abroad. I gave him 500 pesos (S$17). A kid was called in to buy several bottles of gin and soft drinks from the store. My brother and his friends settled down on a corner of the yard by the coconut tree to start the partying that was to last for two days. During the same two days, people would be coming in and out of the house, and there would be endless drinking and eating in our small living room. After my oldest brother and his family arrived from their own hometown, there was more drinking and partying.

My daughters' insistent tugging at my hands pulled me back into the present. They wanted to open my luggage and look for their *pasalubong*. I sat down with the girls upstairs and opened my suitcases. I did not take out any of the personal items I had for them, but instead, I took out the candies and the soaps and started distributing some of the chocolates to them and the guests.

I was careful not to give out all of it, because I knew that more people would be coming by, and I wanted to have little things to share with them when they did. My aunts and cousins would visit sooner or later. I laid out the second hand clothes that I brought home.

My mother and my big sister would pick what they wanted first then leave the rest for the other women. I would, in the next two days, be giving out the rest of the chocolates, individual bars of bath soaps, good quality second hand clothes to our cousins and friends. But on that first evening, the apples and grapes and oranges went really fast.

I brought out the packages of Marlboro and Salem cigarettes for my brothers and those went very fast too. My brothers continued drinking, talking and smoking in the yard, deep into the night.

Various relatives and friends continued trickling into the house to visit and my mother was happy to brew more coffee for them. On my third day, I ran out of presents to distribute to the public, but they still came, interested in hearing my story and how I lived in Singapore. And I told them, again and again, and again. I told them how clean, how organised, how different Singapore was. I told them about my employer.

My mother, with whom I had established a new and more loving relationship, starting from my conversion almost two years ago, hovered proudly and happily in the background, interjecting every now and then, to remind me to patch the holes in my story, "Tell them about the food, *Ineng* ..."

My family still called me by my childhood name, *Ineng*, which meant "little girl", and this included my own daughters. None of them called me "mother" at the time, not even Catherine.

Everyone who came by checked me out for physical signs of prosperity and changes in my person but were terribly disappointed. The villagers expected me to gain weight, a definite sign of affluence and well-being. They expected me to be wearing imported items, like gold jewelry and Ray Ban sunglasses. Filipinos love those things.

They said, "You haven't changed much. You look like you just came back from shopping for groceries ..."

Yet, subtly, things have changed in the people's perception of me. Despite lacking in worldly possessions, I was now friendly and informative and they realised they could talk to me.

A lot of the people who came to visit expressed great interest in finding work in Singapore themselves, and asked how I could help them. I made no promises, but right then and there, I decided there were ones amongst them that I would try to help out if I could.

On the fourth day, I breathed easier. My girls and I were now able to spend the day by ourselves. The chocolates and everything else had now been distributed and consumed, and I had some time to relax and cuddle my little ones. All during the last three days, the three girls barely left my side. I gave them their real presents — their toothbrushes, umbrellas, extra allowances, toys. I brought Catherine a stuffed, yellow teddy bear as big as herself.

On my fifth day, the children and I walked around the village and visited older aunts and uncles to pay my respects. I did this upon my mother's urging. She deemed it important that I show myself in their presence. It was customary for younger people to do this; otherwise, you would never hear the end of it. These were the relatives who couldn't visit because they were either bedridden or too old to leave the house.

So I went, and because I was also expected to bring them a present, I gave my elders a small amount of cash. The practice was perfectly acceptable. This they accepted reluctantly, modestly, but with joy.

A few tight-fisted relatives disapproved of my generous nature. They knew I wasn't dripping with cash, and they suspected that I haven't been saving money for myself.

They were right, in a way. I did send most of what I earned back to my mother, for the family's daily needs, or to pay off whatever debts she may have incurred, and to help my brothers or sister when they came to her for hand-outs. But the fact remained that this was my family I was helping. And my mother, sensing how hard I must have worked, saved every peso that could be saved, and bought enough land to house the whole family — and this she did in only two years.

As far as I was concerned, I considered all this money well spent. Of course, others would beg to differ.

Like one of my cousins, a part-time, five-six moneylender who had turned me down for a loan two-and-a-half years ago. He now accosted me about the way I spent my hard-earned money, saying, "If you kept sending your money to your mother, you'll end up with nothing. Smarten up, kid!"

I did not think he had any right to judge my actions. It wasn't his money I was sending to my mother. When I needed help, he had refused me. So I smiled and told him, "Relax, *Kuya*, remember, I can't carry any of this money to my grave."

He looked at me blankly for a few seconds, but when he finally understood what I just said, he swore under his breath and walked away.

I loved recounting that scene. It brought much laughter each time I re-told it, especially to my mother and brother.

On my sixth day home, I came down with a cold and fever. It could be due to exhaustion, or a sudden change of climate. Maricel and Maricar started to go back to their old routine — hanging out with friends — but checked in on me every now and then. Catherine stayed close by my side, sitting near the bed and playing with her new toys.

At one point, she fell asleep beside me. It was a very endearing scene, watching her clutch her new teddy bear while napping beside me. When she woke up, she saw that her sisters were back. Catherine scolded them soundly for not being more conscientious and caring about their mother. I was smiling to myself the whole time. These recollections I hoarded like little gems in my memory box.

I spent a whole month in the Philippines before going back to

Singapore — a month that was over far too soon. This time, I decided to hire a village jeepney so that the whole family — my mother, my sister, my brothers and their wives, and the girls — could see me off. The jeepney was loaded up with a picnic lunch and drinks for everybody.

Our driver parked at the airport's public lot and everybody walked with me to the immigration gates. I kissed everyone goodbye, then slowly walked away without looking back.

I heard Maricel start to cry. Maricar and Catherine followed suit. My mother called out a blessing.

I walked on, faster and faster; farther and farther away from them, my heart beating as if it would explode inside my chest. I thought I would pass out. But I did not stop.

Because if I stopped, if I looked back, I would never leave.

And I needed to go. My dreams for my little ones had only been half-fulfilled.

SHARING THE DREAM

My life in Singapore had taken many turns and I was feeling good about myself. I was making enough money to support my family. I was debt-free, and I had a little bit left over for my personal expenses. I had acquired a huge network friends, and I had good references. I had gone home, seen my daughters, spent time with my family, and grown close to my mother.

But one observation nagged me. While back home, I had been reminded of the poverty and lack of opportunities that people in my village face. I decided to do my best to help friends and relatives whenever I could. I noted the names of women whose family would benefit from them getting dollar-earning job. I promised my brothers and sister that I would help them send each of their first-borns to college.

Let me tell you, good intentions are easy to come by; putting them into practice is always harder than you think. Never forget the human factor. The first person I tried to bring into Singapore was my childhood friend, Imelda. We grew up together in the city. She used to work at my Aunt's grocery store during the weekends and went to school on weekdays. She and I were close buddies, a you-and-me partnership against our well-heeled, same-aged cousins who weren't very nice to us. We were the poor relations.

After graduating from high school, Imelda kept working for our Aunt Paula, and I went off to college. She came back to live in the village after getting married, and at one point, our lives intersected again when both of us became unemployed single parents living in the parental home and dependent on our families for support. If there was anyone in real need of my help, it was Imelda. I loved her like a sister, and even though I wasn't any good at communicating this, we both knew that our friendship was alive and burning. Much as I had expected, when the jeepney I was riding in entered the village, Imelda was there, standing by the roadside, welcoming me home. I will always remember how she visited me at home, carrying her youngest child, before the dust left behind by the jeepney settled back on the road. Imelda told me to keep her in mind if ever a job opening came up in Singapore. I assured her that when it happened, she'd be the first to hear about it.

After a few months back in Singapore, an opportunity to help Imelda presented itself. Grandma Han had taken sick and the family needed someone to help with the housekeeping. The family asked if I could recommend someone I knew from the Philippines. I was only too happy to do so and promised them I would get the best person to look after Grandma's house. I immediately contacted Imelda. To my great annoyance, however, I found out that Imelda had recently remarried and was now reluctant to leave her new husband. What could I say? Better luck next time.

My next choice was Nenita, another childhood friend in the city. She and I grew up together away from our families in the city, and having this in common probably drew us closer. Nenita was the eldest in a brood of six and had graduated from college. She was working as a filing clerk when we last spoke. When I called, Nenita was interested and ready to go. My Mumsy applied for the work permit, sent her the papers and air ticket and we waited. Word came back that Nenita couldn't leave because her father just had a heart attack, and was in a very serious condition. Soon after that, Grandma's heart problems also landed her in the hospital. We now had two people, both in need of Nenita's presence, and both very sick. Nenita opted to stay back in the Philippines, in order to look after her ailing father. It was a very frustrating time for me because I knew how much Grandma's family needed help, but I also understood that Nenita was hard pressed to choose between her father and a stranger.

The family and I decided to wait it out. We had to make do without

Nenita. Weeks passed. Grandma's condition got worse. In Nenita's parallel universe, things weren't getting better either. About five months later, Grandma passed away. Nenita's father died soon after. After a period of mourning, Nenita was ready to come to Singapore. She still had the air ticket and work permit. I had to explain to Nenita that the family no longer needed a housekeeper. Nenita was not very happy. The whole village was talking about her, she told me. They were saying she had been faked. I could feel her frustration, but I could do nothing about it. I told her to sit tight, and meanwhile, straighten out those who were talking behind her back. If that didn't work, I would go home and personally slap each of them using Nenita's employment papers.

I reminded Nenita patiently, "It wasn't your fault that you had to stay back in the Philippines when you were supposed to leave. But a person who gets faked is someone who has paid a lot of money to get a job abroad but never got one. You didn't have to spend anything to get your work permit approved. You haven't lost anything."

I went down a long list of people whom I promised to help find work in Singapore. The next one was my cousin, Santa, who had once worked in Hong Kong for 10 months as a maid. She wanted to work in Singapore, although she did not really need a job, since she and her husband were operating a profitable grocery store in Manila. Santa was my mother's niece — my first cousin. She grew up with my older siblings, and used to come stay with us when I was a child. Before she got married, she was even roped in at various points to look after me. I used to be terrified of her. She had watched me cast aside my opportunities when I was young, and naturally, she hadn't been impressed. Santa had expressed her disapproval before, and I think she secretly believed that I would never amount to anything. With her, I felt I had to prove myself. I wanted to be able to say, see here, I straightened my life out. I brought her in to work for Kwang and Bee Leng. This was after the birth of their first son, Ming Chou.

You'd think getting her to Singapore was easy. The family wanted her; Santa said she would come; the work permit was ready; the air ticket was in her hands, but what was she still doing back in the Philippines? For reasons unknown to me, she was taking her sweet time coming to Singapore. Kwang and Bee Leng desperately needed a maid, but Santa dug in her heels back home. She couldn't make up her mind about coming. Sure, she liked the idea of working abroad, but when it came to the crunch, I think she couldn't bear the thought of leaving her children alone. I was impatient. Her children were old enough to look after themselves. The two younger ones were already in college and the elder two were gainfully employed. We waited and waited. Santa arrived eventually, and not a minute too soon.

Since then, I had often questioned my sanity for bringing her over. Santa and Bee Leng, two strong-willed women, spent some time learning to work together. I became the receptacle of unexpressed frustrations from both sides. It worked out eventually. Santa doted on Ming Chou and loved playing the grandma. She and Bee Leng became good friends. Santa and I, too, grew closer, and although she preferred going to a Catholic church, we still found time to go out together during our days off. Santa went to St Francis Xavier in the Serangoon area and had her own group of friends, many of whom, admirably, she still kept contact with up to this day.

A few months later, a couple from the Marine Parade Christian Fellowship approached me to ask for help in hiring a maid from the Philippines. I tried to help Imelda one more time. When I called to ask her whether she was still interested, Imelda told me she couldn't make it. She was pregnant again.

So I wrote to one of my friends, Elvira, from the same village. Like me, she had been the leftover half of yet another unhappy marriage. She had three children and no income, and was living with her parents and siblings. Her older sister, Merlita, had just returned from working as a housekeeper in Saudi Arabia. As it turned out, Elvira, too, couldn't make it, so the job was offered to Merlita instead. We started the process of hiring Merlita, but she kept stalling for time. Months passed. By this time, Nenita had arrived in Singapore to take my place at Mumsy's. I was then waiting for my work visa to Vancouver.

In the meantime, I helped Merlita's employer look after their little boy. Merlita, who had access to the phone, was never around when I called her, or her family would make up one excuse or another. I eventually found out through the grapevine that Merlita was holding out for another position in Saudi Arabia, and would have given up the offer here had that worked out. Hearing this made me very unhappy, because she was not the person I wanted to help in the first place. Now I had to work in her place, when I should be spending more time training Nenita at Mumsy's.

As this mess was all my fault, I discussed the options with Evelyn, Merlita's waiting employer, and we decided that we would give her two weeks' grace. Either she get here then, or the job would go to someone else. I communicated this to Merlita gravely — and it worked. She was in Singapore in five days.

Right after her arrival, Merlita asked her bosses for a raise, and I was totally embarrassed by what she did. I visited her once, and after that, I never spoke to her again. Merlita eventually made her way to Toronto, and later helped Elvira find a job in Hong Kong. The latter afterwards married an American and migrated to the US.

Evangeline was the only one who didn't give me any trouble whatsoever. She was Arlin's niece and I helped her upon Arlin's request. Thankfully, she arrived on time; her employers were happy with her, and I left Singapore knowing she was working in a good household.

After Evangeline, I gave up trying to help other people find employers altogether. It was too stressful and too much trouble. Based on these experiences, I realised that if someone really wanted to go abroad, she would find ways to get there, without any assistance from me.

Most of the people I helped did not do too badly, though, as I'm happy to report. Nenita followed me to Canada, and through hard work, was able to send her younger sister through college, and help her brothers financially. Merlita went off to Toronto where all her daughters have joined her. Santa and three of her children are now living and working in Vancouver.

After Singapore, I decided to concentrate on helping my own family. I talked often to my nieces and nephews, encouraging them to study hard. After all, I had helped finance their university education. Even that one did not turn out the way I expected. Only two out of five people I helped send to college graduated. Three got married before finishing school, and one got involved with the wrong crowd. I have since concluded that I could always dream for others, but it is up to them how badly they want that dream realised.

HIKING THE NANNY TRAIL

Working as a maid in a foreign country is like exploring the Amazon jungle without a map. All you see before you are unmarked trails, but you know that all you have to do is go in a straight line. You go in, you grope your way through the undergrowth, take pains to avoid the leeches and the crocodiles, keep an eye out for the bogs and the sand traps... In a few years or so, you will have crossed this jungle, and there on the other side, your family will be waiting to welcome you back. If you're fortunate, you'll go home happy and fulfilled, and your life will be better than when you started. You'll be richer in material things, and you would have gained friends and wisdom.

Janet Munoz is one such person. Janet came to Singapore in 1986 under the employ of Mr and Mrs Francis Lim. The family has two children and lives in Serangoon Gardens. The Lims separated in 1989, but Janet continued working for Mr Lim, looking after his children and his home. In effect, she became the surrogate mother to both his children. She even took them to St Francis Xavier Church to attend mass every Sunday. That same year, Janet went home to Makati in the Philippines to marry her jeepney driver boyfriend. After the wedding, she came back to Singapore and worked for another two years.

With her savings, Janet's husband bought his own jeepney and a motorised passenger tricycle. He wanted her to return home for good, and when she declined, he took up with another woman, just to spite her. Janet was beside herself with anger and disappointment, but eventually, she forgave him and went home for a visit. To avoid further disagreements, she decided to go home more often.

By the early 90s, Janet started staying back for longer periods in Makati. Her charges were now teenagers, and did not need her full-time care. Finally, in 1995, she gave birth to their first child, a boy, and in 1998, they had another baby girl. With financial help from her boss, Janet and her husband started two businesses in the city — a purified water-refilling station and an automated laundry employing eight people. Janet is what one would consider a success back home. She now makes enough to support her elderly parents and is helping to finance the building of a Catholic chapel in her parents' hometown in Cagayan.

Janet still comes to Singapore whenever her Singaporean family needs her. In fact, her husband and two children, Francis Lim and his two children, and Janet's six relatives who are now working as maids in Singapore, had become one extended family. Janet had brought Mr Lim's two children home to the Philippines for a two-month vacation in 2004, and more recently, Janet's husband and two children stayed with the Lims in Singapore for three weeks.

Every Sunday after mass, regardless of whether Janet is here or away, her bunch of relatives would congregate at Mr Lim's house. They would cook Filipino food for themselves and for the Lims — a weekly ritual enjoyed by the entire family.

Janet Munoz was one of the luckier ones. Not all stories come with happy endings. For some others, the only thing they brought back was bitterness. Or worse, one could even be going home in a wooden casket. Many, in fact, go on working, much like the Energizer bunny; slogging away, all the while promising themselves that they'd stay "just one more year ..."

There is no way of telling how things would turn out. Everyone leaves the Philippines on an equal footing, with our teeth repaired, our health certified, our criminal records cleared, and with the blessings of families and friends. We have the employment contracts. So what could go wrong?

Plenty.

A domestic worker is going away to live an indentured life — not necessarily to our employers — but to our self-imposed plans for the future. We are slaves to our ambitions; to the promises we made to others, to the expectations of our families. In an effort to make good these promises, a domestic worker in a foreign country could become easily depressed, or feel increasingly isolated.

She is haunted by a persistent fear of failure. She worries constantly that she may not be up to the job, and worries endlessly about those she has left behind. Many married women working abroad make the mistake of hiding their real situations from their families back home. It could be due to pride, or the desire to save their family members from worry.

Whatever the case, many maids do not talk about their homesickness, and neglect to write about the backbreaking work, or in some instances, the unhappy work relations. These women fail to mention how their tears flow into the mop bucket everyday, just thinking about home while they wash the floor. Rather, they send home happy letters, party photos and smiling facsimiles of themselves.

"Don't worry about me, I'm fine." That's the standard refrain. When you hear this, start worrying.

They do not talk about how long it took to cobble together those thousands of pesos they send home each time, to get the children through school, or to buy that new TV, dining table, etc; or to repair the leaking roof.

Instead, they write, "Don't worry about me, I'm fine."

Many maids — mothers — will try to erase their guilt and longing for their children by sending them Barbie dolls and chocolates and walkmans in lieu of themselves. They ships home boxes filled with canned food, Nike sneakers and Levi pants.

A maid won't tell her children, "I'm sorry I had to go away, but I miss you and I love you and I'm doing all these things for you. I promise that one day we'll be together again." She assumes that they already know this. All she says is, "Be good children. Listen to your father/grandma/ auntie. Don't worry about me, I'm fine".

Many of these children, as a result of being deprived of motherly care, show proneness to illness, failure in school, juvenile delinquency and aggressive behaviour. Others have been observed to engage in extravagant and wasteful expenditures.

A wife also deprives her husband of her company, and in a few cases, her prolonged absence breaks up the family. Some men couldn't accept the sudden role-reversal. Suddenly, the man becomes a house-husband, in-charge of looking after the children, and living off the wife's income. He is no longer the breadwinner, and consequently, he feels that his manhood is at stake. This, and the lack of female companionship, often drives a husband to infidelity.

A foreign domestic then becomes nothing more than a cash cow — someone who becomes a receptacle of resentment whenever she fails at her task. I have met many such women, such as my friend Gloria, who eventually killed herself. Or Maximina, whom I met recently in Singapore.

Maximina's story caused me much grief, because hers was a story so commonly told. Maximina had already been working in Singapore for about two years when I first met her. She helped her husband, a fisherman, put their two kids through college — an expensive undertaking. Recently, her husband started complaining of poor catches, and asked for more money for the children's school expenses. Maximina, who had just finished her two-year contract, was all set to go home for a holiday. So she held off going back, and cashed in her air ticket instead. This money was then promptly sent back to her husband. From that time on, the demand for cash came fast and furious, so much so that Maximina was forced to borrow money from her employers. Her husband claimed it wasn't enough, and when Maximina failed to send any more, he refused to speak to her. She tried desperately to contact him. Finally, Maximina called her sister-in-law, to find out what was happening. But all her sister-in-law said was, "Well, you knew you had to send more money."

Maximina replied that she didn't have any more money to spare, and asked in despair, "Perhaps I should go out into the streets and work as a prostitute?"

The sister-in-law answered, "If that's what you have to do, go ahead."

Looking at Maximina and hearing her story was very upsetting. Then it hit me — one of these days, God forbid, Maximina may just choose to take the easy way out, like Gloria did; like so many women whose desperation led to suicide. When that happens, you usually hear of it in the newspapers, with headlines such as "Maid found dead at void deck", or "Maid jumped from HDB flat". I prayed that such a day would never come for Maximina. I told her that her family would just have to make do with what she could afford, and that she should be firm and honest and stop making a martyr of herself, because that will not solve the problem.

I felt an uncontrollable urge to march back home, look up Maximina's husband, and yell some sense into him.

Such problems are not solely the domain of the married domestic. The single maid, too, has her share of burdens. The only difference is that she does not have children to think about — but that's only one worry less.

Kinship has its merits, but it could also act as ball and chain around your ankle. Inevitably, it falls to the single, unmarried daughter to provide for elderly parents. Every Filipino woman working in another country, married or not, is worth her weight in gold to her family in the Philippines. That's a fact.

According to the latest Philippine Overseas Employment Agency numbers, there are about five million Filipinos currently employed abroad. Most of these workers hold valid contracts. A big percentage of these workers are women. Until 2003, bank and remittance office records indicate that workers send home an average of US$8.5 million a year.

But these are only official records. Consider the fact that many workers personally bring back cash, or send back cash via friends and relatives, and the final figure you get is a much larger one.

Domestic workers, which included me at one point, helped keep the Philippine economy afloat. We clothed, educated and raised our children in absentia, at great cost to ourselves.

Hiking the nanny trail is not an easy job, even though the rewards are good for those who survive the course.

Would I do it all over again? Could I leave my children again? The answer is "yes", because I don't have a choice.

"Hey, don't worry about me, I'm fine."

TIME TO GO

How shall I go in peace and without sorrow? Nay, not without a wound in the spirit shall I leave this city...

Too many fragments of spirit have I scattered in these streets, and too many are the children of my longing that walk naked among these hills, and I cannot withdraw from them without a burden and an ache.

It is not a garment I cast off this day, but a skin that I tear with my own hands...

Yet I cannot tarry longer.

The sea that calls all things unto her calls me, and I must embark.

For to stay, though the hours burn in the night, is to freeze and crystallize and be bound in a mould.

Fain would I take with me all that is here, but how shall I?

A voice cannot carry the tongue and the lips that gave it wings...

Kahlil Gibran
The Prophet

It was 1987. A buzz was going around the nanny grapevine. Canada is in need of foreign hired help. Like their Singaporean counterparts, Canadian women now prefer to work outside the home, and have someone else look after their children. Many of the Filipino maids I knew had applied to Canada and left the country.

Domestic employment in Canada was a step up from domestic work in Singapore. Not because of the employers, but the way the employment contract was drawn up, and because it offered contract workers a chance to become immigrants.

Domestics were required to work an eight-hour day, on a five-day week, at an hourly minimum wage rate. A nanny still has to live with her employers until she gets her landing status, but room and board are now deducted from her monthly pay.

The big reason that drew these women, including myself, to Canada was that after completing two years of work, a foreign domestic may apply for landing status and bring her family into the country. Like everybody else, that was part of my plan.

"Give me your poor, your homeless, your huddled masses yearning to breathe free..." The statute of Liberty wasn't in Canada, but to us, it didn't matter that the symbol of freedom belonged to America. As far as we were concerned, Canada was as close as it gets to the promised land, and that was good enough for us.

It was the dream that carried us through — the dream of a better life, financial freedom, of growth and personal development.

After I arrived in Vancouver, I realised how little my folks back home really knew about these places. Canada, just by itself, was a place so huge it spans four different time zones, and the whole of the Philippines could conveniently fit into a corner of British Columbia. A distant cousin from my village once requested that I drop off a letter to his relatives in Toronto. I said I'd love to, but Toronto was five hours away by plane from where I lived. It was a revelation to them.

Although there was no question about my following the migrant trail to the West, I wasn't in a hurry to leave Singapore. I loved this country, and had I been single and free of responsibilities, I would probably have stayed on in this place. Going away would be painful, I knew, but I was prepared for it.

Experience has taught me not to hold on to anything too tightly, because nothing lasts forever, including pain. Once in Canada, I knew my love-sickness for Singapore will fade away. I just have to survive the transition.

I had my plans all laid out and it was only a matter of time before I pick up my bags and leave. I had by then developed a high level of trust in God, a spiritual belief that He would lead me to the right place, at the right time. Some people call that living by faith. But I also believe in prodding and nudging things along, towards the direction that I think

God will have me go. I feel it is necessary to combine faith with solid earthly effort.

It's a Filipino thing. As our elders say, *"Nasa Diyos ang awa, nasa tao ang gawa."* — God provides the blessings, but man does the work.

My chance came when I heard that recruiters from Able Nannies were coming down to Singapore to hire workers for Vancouver in British Columbia. I did not remember exactly how I learned of their arrival. I probably saw an ad in *The Straits Times Classifieds*. Anyway, on the stated day, there they were in a downtown hotel's meeting room: Linda Rogers and two other representatives from the Able Nannies Employment Agency, handing out application forms to an excited group of Filipino domestics.

Once again, I was applying for a job and hoping for the best. Only this time, I was not as desperate as I had been two and a half years ago. I had no doubts that I would get to Vancouver. It was an opportunity of a lifetime, and when Linda Rogers arrived, I recognised it as a sign that my universe — as they say — was unfolding as it should.

Why do I say that?

Because the image of Vancouver had been in my mind since I was a displaced child living in the city. One day, reading my aunt's copy of *Reader's Digest*, I chanced upon a picture of Vancouver in the fall. It was captioned, "Autumn in Vancouver", and it showed the trees in full colour from maroon and gold, to yellow and green. I was floored.

I was 10 years old then. I didn't know leaves could do that! In the Philippines, everything stayed green throughout the year, although in the sunnier months, they could turn brown, but that was all.

I promised myself that one day, I was going there to see those leaves for myself. That picture never left my mind. It somehow stayed in my memory, and as years went by, became a vision that turned into a beacon, signaling for me to fulfill my promise.

I attended the Able Nannies' information session, filled out the application form, and paid the S$100 recruitment fee. Then I sat there and waited to be interviewed. Canada's Foreign Domestic Movement Program had less restrictive requirements then. But we were advised that married women with more than one child stood a lesser chance of landing a job in Canada. Linda Rogers told us that the government was not keen on having a domestic bring in a big family, in case she became incapable of supporting them later. Linda didn't say it in so many words, but let's read between the lines — lie if you want the job.

Déjà vu.

I had to deal with the same question once again. Marital status? Lying was easier this time, because all my papers already proved that I was single, and all I had to do was live the same lie once more.

I closed my eyes to calm myself, forcing down the guilt that was rising up my throat. Lie one last time, I told myself. I knew such a lie would have implications for me, when it comes to sponsoring my family later.

But heck, I'll cross that bridge when I come to it.

As part of the application package, we were asked to write a letter to prospective employers in Vancouver. We were asked to describe ourselves, our interests, our special abilities, and what we hoped to achieve in Canada. I wrote mine, describing myself as a good cook and housekeeper who loved children, but who was only an average swimmer. Linda Rogers loved it. She held it up to other applicants as an example of a friendly and well-written nanny-to-employer letter.

A few months later, I heard back from Linda, who told me that they have found me an employer — a couple, both lawyers, from North Vancouver, with two pre-school children and a baby. As part of the hiring process, I corresponded with my future employers, exchanging pictures and letters until we felt comfortable with each other.

I had taken the first step. Now for the next one. One night after dinner, I sat Mumsy down and told her about my plans. I reminded her that Nenita was ready to take my place. Mumsy took my announcement very well. She had always been understanding and supportive.

All we needed to do now was obtain a new work permit for Nenita. I contacted Nenita and told her to get ready.

Meanwhile, my papers were being processed. My new employers had sent my papers to the Canadian High Commission in Singapore, and soon after, I was given another set of forms to fill up. That done, I was required to go through an extensive medical examination. This was to confirm that I was physically and mentally fit for work, and to assess if I could, in the future, become an immigrant or citizen of Canada. You have to admire the country's long-term planning. I suppose it wouldn't be easy to send someone away once she was already living there.

I asked around for a suitable doctor, and what do you know, the nanny community had very definite ideas about the matter. I was told to avoid this or that doctor on the list of approved physicians, as he poked around and stroke you too much, and the modest Filipino woman did not like that.

I went to someone recommended by a Singaporean friend, and he was as good as I heard he was. The good doctor asked me a series of questions, checked the corresponding little boxes in the form I presented to him, examined my stomach over my clothes and then sent me over to the X-Ray clinic. That was it. He sent the completed medical form to the Canadian High Commission himself.

The next thing I knew, the Canadian High Commission wrote to say that I had passed the medical examination, and they were waiving the interview. All I needed to do now was wait for my visa to arrive.

When Nenita arrived two weeks later, we spent some time together, rediscovering our friendship. I had the chance then to teach her some of the dishes that Grandma had taught me. I helped her navigate and interpret cooking instructions from the different cookbooks in Mumsy's collection. I trained her to perform other household duties the way Mumsy wanted them done.

That time is now somewhat hazy in my memory, but what I remembered vividly was her frustration and mine as I demonstrated how to clean the house and tidy up the kitchen after meals. I wanted her to do it precisely my way.

I realised soon enough, however, just how different our way of doing things were, after she threw a wok into the sink full of soapy water, in annoyance. I was reminded that we were no longer lost kids back home. We had both grown up, and I should let her do it her own way, as long as she achieved the same result.

I supposed I was feeling a bit guilty about abandoning my Mumsy and the kids, and felt I had to make sure I was leaving them in the care of a worthwhile substitute.

One of the things I drilled into Nenita's brain was to never to let the boys fight, or more specifically, never to give Marc a chance to murder his little brother. I warned her that if it ever happened, she should also arrange for her own funeral. I was exaggerating, of course, but that did not faze her. Nenita said confidently, "Leave the matter to me."

I asked her to promise that she would look after the family well, especially Mumsy, and to take no shit from anyone outside of the extended household.

I recognised how faithfully she followed my instructions when I came back for a visit a year later — when Bossy proudly and affectionately reported, "This maid, she is more fierce than you!" Hearing that from the boss was proof that Nenita was doing a fine job. Nenita's training went well.

One day, my visa arrived. It was time to go. I went home to the Philippines for a month to let everyone know I was going to Canada. I spent most of that time with my three girls, explaining to them in detail my future plans.

I promised them that this time, I would not be staying away for too long. Afterwards, I went back to Singapore and boarded a plane for Vancouver.

I left Singapore for Vancouver on June 26, 1988.

Mumsy, Bossy, Marc, Kenny and Nenita went to see me off. I cried a little bit while giving them my final hugs. I knew I would miss my two little boys very much. But I also knew that Nenita would look after them the way I had trained her to.

In the meantime, Canada waited. At long last, I was marching towards my manifest destiny.

SINGAPORE,
ONE MORE TIME

January, 2005.

As my plane descended towards Changi International Airport, I looked down through my window to take in the scenery. I last visited the country 15 years ago. There it is, still green, and perhaps still as clean as ever, my Singapore — a universe unto itself. Its current leader is Prime Minister Lee Hsien Loong, the elder son of Mr Lee Kuan Yew. What is Singapore like today? This is what I've come back to find out.

I stepped out into the humid tropical air, and got into a waiting cab. I will be staying at the Copthorne Orchid Hotel. All along the Pan Island Expressway, I craned my neck to watch the roadside scenery rushing by. The trees seem to be so much taller now; the branches wider, the flowering hedges higher. There were rain trees and royal palms all along the various roads on the way downtown, bougainvilleas and red sealing wax palms. The apartment buildings are now more colourful, with splashes of green, teal, blue, purple, orange or brown, in contrast to the monochromatic beige I remembered from years ago.

I checked into the hotel and walked down to the shop to pick up a copy of *The Straits Times*. I wanted to re-acquaint myself with the place before facing my Singaporean "relatives".

The next morning, I hopped onto the hotel shuttle bus and got off at Tangs Department Store. There, I changed some Canadian money into Singapore dollars, and ate fish porridge at the basement food court at Lucky Plaza. The porridge, washed down with a glass of iced coca cola, was as good as it was 15 years ago. After the meal, I walked up and down the mall and examined the shops.

LUCKY PLAZA

Lucky Plaza looked the same at first glance, but I realised how much it has changed upon closer inspection. *Pinoy* maids had always loved hanging out at this mall, sitting on ledges, on benches, on every vacant corner, walking up and down the escalators, and eating at its fast food joints.

Their presence must have been really good business for some stores, but not for others. Twenty years ago, stores at Lucky Plaza were all operated by Singaporeans, selling mainly jewelry, shoes, clothes, beauty and electronic products. Most shops still offer the same items, but they were not as numerous as before.

The local merchants seemed to have taken heed of the customer mix, and have conceded to supply what the immigrant community demanded. Many shops now cater to the homesick Filipino worker, selling basic items like pre-paid phone cards, bags of crunchy pork rind, *Fita* crackers, canned food like sardines and pickled vegetables, candies, green and ripe mangoes, clothes shipped from the Philippines, magazines, lotions and shampoos, as well as various art and craft pieces.

Several restaurants on the fourth and fifth floors now serve popular Filipino dishes like *sinigang, pancit,* and *lumpia.* Remittance and cargo offices compete to help send the workers' money and goods home to the Philippines. There are also a number of employment agencies offering the services of maids from the Philippines, Thailand or Indonesia. These establishments were non-existent during my time.

The whole mall is still teeming with Filipino women on weekends, mostly domestic workers, I suspect, but there are now far fewer men. The construction boom is over and the demand for male workers is consequently weaker.

But more than just the changed physical landscape was the change in people's habits. While walking down Orchard Road, I notice that almost everyone — maid, student, shopper — was carrying a mobile phone. Almost every maid I met was holding one, and was either talking into it or punching in a text message. Groups are noticeably quieter because instead of chatting, many of them are now occupied with these modern communication gadgets. I noticed the same thing when I was at the airport.

After spending a day at Orchard Road, I went back to the hotel, ordered Hainanese chicken rice for dinner, then phoned Bee Leng to tell her where I was.

KWANG & BEE LENG

The next day, Bee Leng came and picked me up. I was going to stay with them for two weeks. Kwang and Bee Leng live in a big, three-storey house designed by his younger brother, Loke Kwang (or Ah Chai), who is now an accomplished architect.

The house has French windows that look out into the garden. One on side of this garden was Bee Leng's collection of bonsai and tropical plants. From the kitchen windows, one can see her herb garden, as well as the banana, papaya and palm trees that discreetly screen the house from the prying eyes of neighbours. Bordering the front yard are various types of flowering trees.

The ground floor of the house is divided into the living room, the front room, the spacious dining room, the big kitchen, and a guest room. The living room opens out into the garden. This part of the garden features a small pond with lotus plants and gurami fish. Bee Leng says the gurami keep the mosquito population down by feeding on their larvae in the pond. The lotus plant has one single but amazingly pretty purple flower. There's also a cactus collection, an old wooden swing and several pieces of lawn furniture.

Inside, a spiral staircase goes up to the second and third floors, where the family bedrooms are located. At the base of this staircase is a pond that's home to a number of colourful koi fish. The second floor balcony faces the front yard, which displays a collection of bougainvillea bushes in full bloom.

The family owns five computers. The Han children, like most

modern kids, love spending long hours in front of their computers. Bee Leng had the machines moved downstairs from the children's bedrooms, to prevent the computer from cutting into the kids' study time and sleeping hours.

Kwang, the "Overachieving Hotshot", now works as Editor of *The Straits Times*. Bee Leng has stopped working a few years ago to devote more time to raising the family, but keeps herself busy by volunteering with her dog therapy group. Bee Leng and her three dogs visit homes for terminally ill people and the mentally disabled at least twice a week. A soprano, she also sings with a world-class choir. The couple now practices yoga regularly, although Kwang does so more religiously.

Bee Leng and Kwang's three children, Ming Chou, Yu Shan, and Yu Shi, are now teenagers. Ming Chou was their only child when I left Singapore. He is currently serving National Service, and seems to be enjoying himself. Yu Shan is in her third year of secondary school and Yu Shi is in the first year. Both girls play competitive ping-pong for their school. All three kids are avid fans of the Japanese cartoon art, manga and anime, and spend whatever free time they could surf the net or exchanging updates with other manga fans through cyberspace. Anime, Bee Leng explains, is the film version, while manga is the printed one.

Bee Leng runs the household with competent help from Riza, her Filipino maid of 11 years. Riza is a gentle and hardworking woman who does not talk very much, and dotes on Bee Leng's children.

The family has three dogs, a beagle called Muffin; Bonnie, a King Charles cavalier spaniel and a siberian husky named Richter. Can you imagine wearing a wool jacket in a 33°C environment? That's how a husky in Singapore should be feeling. However, Richter adapts to the warm climate by growing less hair and shedding whatever he does not need.

The dogs and I get along famously, except when I hang out in the kitchen. Muffin the beagle does not like that. It probably was her territory and I felt like an interloper. That dog would stand in front of me, fix me with a mean stare, wrap her two front legs around one of mine, and start humping it. I thought that was so weird. Riza later explained that Muffin, an alpha female, does this whenever she feels jealous or threatened. The only thing – person – that scares Muffin was the family's Indian gardener, Ajez. So, each time Muffin tries to be mean to me, I would call out Ajez' name and Muffin would run off howling, with her tail between her legs. I never thought teasing a dog could be so much fun.

Bee Leng is the ultimate hostess, and she does her best to make me feel comfortable and welcomed. She is also my source of cultural knowledge. One evening, while we were having dinner at a Szechuan restaurant, I watched her rap the table with two of her fingers after the waitress served us our soup. She noticed me looking and asked if I knew what that meant. I replied, "When playing Poker, that means check the cards."

She laughed and proceeded to tell me this story: A long time ago, a Chinese emperor decided to travel across the country *incognito*, to find out how his subjects were doing. On the road, members of his imperial entourage couldn't openly pay their respects for fear of the Emperor being recognised, so they agreed to rap their fingers on the table each time they wanted to express respect or gratitude to their boss in public.

I remember a shopping trip to Chinatown with Bee Leng and her two girls on the eve of Chinese New Year. The whole place was packed with people like sardines in a can. People were either inching forward or backward, but it was near impossible to walk at normal speed. The streets were decorated with gold, yellow and orange lanterns, as well as huge and ornate designs that depict dragons, lions and other mythological shapes revered by the Chinese.

Dominating the whole display in the middle of the street, sitting on a platform above the traffic, was a huge rooster. Huge red and orange buntings radiated from the rooster's platform and out into both sides of the road.

The shop owners try to outdo each other in ways that constitute a blatant and shameless assault on the senses — some use loud speakers to hawk their products, other have taped firecracker sounds playing the whole evening, and still others have TV screens showing the latest videos of popular local performers. There were all sorts of items on offer — jades jewellery, calligraphic paintings, kuehs of all sorts, Indonesian rice cakes, bottles and bottles of pineapple tarts, and even Turkish ice cream.

There were also oranges by the truckloads, oranges being the prime symbol of prosperity for the Chinese. You can't visit a house on Chinese New Year without offering at least two oranges as a gift. It remains a sign of good wishes.

One day, we drove to Woodlands to pick up the girls from their friend's house, and I had another attack of the "good ole days". Woodlands, which used to be a bustling construction site 20 years ago, is now a big, sprawling town with parks, businesses, schools and impressive high-rise buildings.

This was the place my friend Arlin and his buddies had built. It was where their barracks once stood — a row of make-shift wooden complexes where foreign men entertained their foreign girlfriends; where the poem I once wrote for *The Straits Times* — the one that gave voice to their transient and forbidden love lives — was displayed on the walls of every unit.

On the first day of Chinese New Year, Kwang drove us to Sentosa Island for the Garden Show. Sentosa today is a fully developed resort connected to the mainland by a causeway. The tiny island is now home to top-notch hotels, golf courses, theme parks, restaurants, souvenir shops and huge picnic areas. I marveled at what 15 years could do to a place.

Another area that had been totally transformed was Punggol. To my mind, Punggol was a sleepy town — home to small-time farmers and one of the best chilli crab restaurants around. But when I suggested a trip to Punggol for some crabs, Bee Leng informed me that the funky little restaurant with the wooden tables and chairs have long since been re-located to the East Coast seafood centre. Somehow, that killed the magic for me.

MUMSY & THE BOYS

Towards the weekend, I called Mumsy and arranged to meet with the family at Church.

Mumsy and the boys now live in a three-bedroom HDB flat in Bedok. It was a two-storey unit, with three bedrooms upstairs, and a living, dining and storeroom downstairs alongside the kitchen area. The thing that surprised me most was the fact that Mumsy now has a dog, a schnauzer named Phoebe. She also has rows of potted plants, arranged in a terraced wooden structure, along the outside corridor, just below the dining room windows. We didn't use to have pets or plants back at Eunos Crescent.

As we sat and talked about the changes that had occurred, the years in between started to peel away, revealing in its place the easy familiarity of old. Once again, sitting in front of me, was the Mumsy I had left 15 years ago — the same affection, the same warmth. Mumsy herself had put on a few extra pounds, but she retains the same pretty face; the same twinkle in her eye. Always a good dresser, Mumsy still delights in elegant wear, but now also wears a stylish pair of dangling earrings, which hung three inches down from her lobes. I told her I don't remember seeing her wear earrings like that before. She laughed and responded, "I guess I've become more vain in my old age."

Bossy passed away from cancer in 1996 and Mumsy opted for an early retirement in 2004. She now actively serves as a church volunteer, teaching in Sunday School at the Marine Parade Christian Centre.

Kenny Aw is now almost 24. He drives a car, and is his mother's

constant escort, driver and errands man. He had finished National
Service with a rank of Sergeant, and will be graduating from his course
in computer engineering in 2006. A very smart kid, my erstwhile
little guy. He has also acquired a girlfriend, a cheerful young woman
named Jolin. He hasn't grown as tall as I had hoped he would, but
that's understandable. He has always been a very intense, hardworking
young person, and possibly, all his energies had been channeled into
nurturing his mental abilities.

Marc Aw is now 26 years old, still as friendly, gregarious and very
bright, a travel bug with a taste for adventure. We had a long chat when
I first visited and I found him still as enjoyable a company as when
he was little. He works as a flight steward for Singapore Airlines, and
according to his mother, was a devoted and loving son. Mumsy said
that the first thing Marc does upon disembarking in a strange city was
to call his mother to say he has landed safely. I feel very proud of both
my boys.

GRANDPA & THE GIRLS

Grandpa is a healthy 70, still living in the old East Coast Road home.
He seems happy enough living by himself in a house full of memories.
At a dinner out with Mumsy, Leng and Heng, Grandpa told me about
his younger days when he was working in a fish processing plant in
Malaysia, and that his and Grandma's was an arranged marriage. They
were betrothed at the age of nine by their parents back in Hainan. He
finally met Grandma when she was 19, when her parents sent her off to
Singapore by boat so that they could finally get married.

Write about my story, he asked. Well, maybe I will. It was such a
romantic story.

The Girls, Leng and Heng, still both single, still as pretty as when I
first met them, now live together in their own flat. As in the olden days,
they still join Mumsy and Grandpa for meals and visits on weekends.
But they professed to miss Grandma's cooking, especially her mutton

sou
visi

T]

st
t(
s

The family sold the apartment in 1995 to ou
whose son got married that same year.
As I walked towards the apartment b
to make sure I was in the right place. B
now, but it has acquired a new c
running along the width of the
lot have now been planted
The concrete circle in th
longer there. The old
with faux marble
People to sit o
were all gon
gargantu
are di

with o...
worship leader with my old Filipino...
a teenaged son. Now, the church has its own Filipino pastor and...
its Filipino service on Sunday afternoons. Bossy's sister-in-law, Auntie
Lena, and her two sons, Kelvin and Melvin, are still members. Kelvin
plays the guitar with other church musicians during services.

EUNOS CRESCENT

After church, we all had lunch together at a Siglap restaurant,
where Mumsy ordered several dishes she knew I would appreciate. We
had the raw fish tossed salad, braised chicken in soy sauce, deep fried
tau foo and fried rice, and eggplant with pork. Later, I requested that
Kenny Aw drop me off at Eunos Crescent, so I could visit Block 23, the
building where we used to live in.

r next-door neighbours,

uilding, I checked the number
lock 23 looks somewhat rundown
at of paint, with blue-green stripes
building. The edges of the old parking
with palm trees and other border plants.
e centre where the boys used to play was no
paths have been upgraded into covered walkways
benches built randomly along its entire length, for
n. The concrete benches and tables at the void decks
e, and in their place were rows of bike racks. The dreaded
n garbage bins of yore are now replaced by smaller ones that
screetly locked and hidden at the bottom of the chutes.

Between Block 23 and Block 22, there's a roofed, circular rest hut, with concrete built-in benches running along its low walls and a concrete table in the middle. I walked behind Block 23 and looked up towards its kitchen windows. There were very few laundry poles out and their loads hang limply in the windless afternoon.

I continued walking around, looking closely at everything, but there wasn't much else to see. Everything looked older, and as I walked away from Block 23 through the parking lot, an unexplainable sadness rose up to engulf me.

I felt like Rip Van Winkle walking on to a vaguely familiar scene. All my old friends were gone. Narcy, Paulita, Tina, Lalay, Rose and Ellen had left a long time ago. I have no idea where every one is, and that's all my fault. I went away and neglected to leave a forwarding address. I let them vanish from my life like so much smoke.

It was as if I had been looking through a tunnel where I saw only the things I wanted to see a long way ahead, and outside that tunnel, nothing of importance could exist. How could I be so wrong?

I walked on to the Eunos Public Market, reading the signs as I went along. The PAP office was still there. Mumsy forewarned me that the market had been moved a few meters away from its former location after it burned down. I went into the market to check it out. The stalls were arranged differently and nothing leaped from my memory. What stood out were its colourful displays of Chinese New year merchandise and decorations. The place felt alien to me. I gave up, and took a bus back to Serangoon Gardens.

THE MAIDS

Three days after my arrival in Singapore, I visited the Embassy of the Philippines along Nassim Road, to meet the new people there and to request for an appointment with the Labour Attaché. Even the Embassy has changed a great deal. Every visitor has now to report to the security office and obtain a visitor's pass, and then required to leave her purse and any electronic devices with the guard. In the old days, everyone just walked through the front door. No checks, no hassle.

This time, I was directed toward the back of the Embassy building. The place has its own lounging area furnished with tables and chairs and even a soft-drink vending machine. The whole area looks less threatening for maids who are waiting to be called in, or just wanted to hang out. There were several windows looking out into the lounge, each manned by labour staff. I approach a window and told them I wanted to see the Labour Attaché.

I was told to wait for a few minutes before being called into the Labour Attaché's office. Mrs Merriam Cuasay, the Labour Attaché, looks like a very busy woman. Her in-tray was overflowing with documents. Various files were also spread out on her desk, but she did make some time for me. I asked her for an interview and we agreed to meet for lunch the next day at Orchard Road.

We met at a Filipino restaurant at Lucky Plaza. We seated ourselves and ordered fried chicken and fish soup combo, plus an additional plate of fried prawns. The manager came and served us a complimentary plate of crunchy pork rinds. Then we settled in to talk about the current status of the maids in Singapore. Mrs Cuasay, who took up her posting in Singapore in 1999 after serving term in Hong Kong, was obviously well informed about the situation of Filipino domestics working in both countries.

According to her, there are currently an estimated 60,000 to 75,000 Filipino maids in Singapore. This, at least, is the official number.

There are a few new regulations with regards to the hiring of foreign domestic workers, added to what had been in effect for years. The Singapore Ministry of Manpower now requires domestics and employers to sign a Ministry-approved contract. The starting salary is S$300, the same as 20 years ago. The maid still has to undergo the twice-a-year pregnancy and Aids tests.

In January, 2005, the minimum age requirement for domestic workers applying for a job in Singapore was raised to 23 years. After April of the same year, these applicants were also required to pass English and Numerology tests.

Singaporean employers must post a bond of S$5,000 and pay a monthly levy of $345 in order to employ a foreign maid. Maids now can stay for over 10 years with the same employer.

In 2004, the Labour Attaché started a well-being department for domestics at her offices at the Philippine Embassy. Once an incident of abuse was reported to the labour office, she dispatches a mobile team to pick up the maid, and her employer is notified. The Labour Attaché will then meet with both parties, together and then separately, to try to work things out between them. If there was any unpaid salary due, the department collects it for the maid. The department is reachable by cell phone 24 hours a day, seven days a week.

When I asked her about the old Philippine Community Centre, she told me that it did not exist anymore. Which was, in fact, a white lie, I guess. The Embassy still maintains a place for runaway domestics, but it is no longer open to the public. Like any regular shelter for abused women, its location and phone numbers are kept confidential. Just as in the West, sanctuaries for abused women are never publicised.

Mrs Cuasay is a woman with a mission. She firmly believes in educating the maids, through orientation seminars before they leave the Philippines, and then through more seminars and outreach programmes in the host country. The more information a worker has, she says, the better her chances of survival in a foreign country. Mrs Cuasay plans to get more involved in the education of outgoing overseas workers when her posting is over.

We both agreed that in many instances, going abroad is not always beneficial in the long run. It could bring misery to both the worker and the family she leaves behind. Once again, I was reminded of Imelda, the woman I met nearly 18 years ago at the Philippine Community Centre. She was one of the run-aways staying at the Centre. Imelda was single, but she carried on her shoulders the responsibility of ensuring a comfortable future for her aging parents. Feeling lost and hopeless after losing her job, Imelda chose to kill herself. There had been many others who took the same route, in every part of the world, in every place where Filipino women go to seek the kind of future denied them in the Philippines. Even in Vancouver, Canada.

Before I left, I stood outside the gates of the Philippine Embassy and offered a short prayer for Imelda. I have long accepted that there was nothing I could have done to help her. I was no longer the young, idealistic person who once believed I could actually help keep women like Imelda alive. That was a delusion. My older self now knows that one can only do her best to assist others, but the rest is up to them.

But I am happy that I made this trip, and that I've renewed my ties with my Singaporean family.

Will I come back here again? Perhaps, if only for a holiday.

In the meantime, *au revoir*, Singapore.

One Last Note ...

A few years ago, I wrote a letter to Canada's immigration authorities telling them of my lie. I apologised and explained my actions. I can now bring my children to Canada if I wished. However, they have chosen their own paths, and I'm still here by myself.

My children have forgiven me for leaving them motherless during their early years. Reading this book will made them understand more fully my motives, I hope. They believed me when I said I did my best under the circumstances, and that I did it for them.

This is the story of my life. It has taken many years for me to get where I am today. It has been a long, arduous, yet necessary, journey. To everyone else, to all my friends who did not know who I really was, let this book be a confession — This is me, warts and all.

And to all the other women who will decide to follow the same road that I took, I hope you will find my experiences helpful, even for a little bit.